0236777

D1760986

GUIDE COLLOMB

This book is due for return on or before the last date shown below.

9

guide collomb

STUBAI ALPS

AND SOUTH TIROL

definitive walking   hut touring   cross country
scrambling and climbing guide

Jeff Williams

West Col

STUBAI ALPS AND SOUTH TIROL

First published in this edition 1991 by
West Col Productions
Goring   Reading   Berks.   RG8 9AA

SBN   906227 51 8

Printed and made in England

Contents

Illustrations

ABBREVIATIONS

approx.	approximately
Äuss.	Äussere, outer
AV	Alpenverein(s)
AVF	Alpenverein guidebook
b.	date of original hut building
B	number of beds in hut
c	circa, approximation (of height)
CAI	Italian Alpine Club
DAV	German Alpine Club
DÖAV	German and Austrian Alpine Club – an amalgamation in 1872, disbanded after 1939
enl.	date of enlargement/alteration to hut
FA.	First ascensionists
FB	Freytag-Berndt (maps)
Gr.	Grosser, larger
h	hour(s)
Hint.	Hintere, rear
IGM	Italian Military maps
Inn.	Innere, inner
Ital.	Italian
KK	Kompasskarten (maps)
Kl.	Kleiner, smaller
km	kilometre(s)
L	left (direction)
m	metre(s)
M	number of mattress places in hut
min.	minutes
Mittl.	Mittlere, middle
Nördl.	Nördliche, northern
ÖAV	Austrian Alpine Club
ÖK	Austrian official map
Östl.	Östliche, eastern
ÖTK(ÖTC)	Austrian Tourist Club
pt.	point on route, spot height on map
PT.	Nearest public transport dropping pt.
R	right (direction)
R.	Route (number)
Rif.	Rifugio (Ital. – hut)
Sekt	Section (of Alpine Club)
Südl.	Südliche/Südlichste, southern/southermost
Tel.	public telephone(number)
TVN	Touristenverein Naturfreunde
UIAA	International Union of Alpine Associations
Vord.	Vordere, nearer
Westl.	Westliche, western

Standard abbreviations for directions, eg. N, S, W, E, NW, SSE.

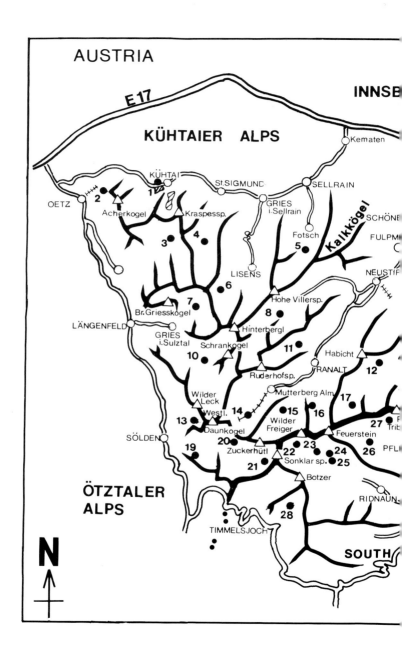

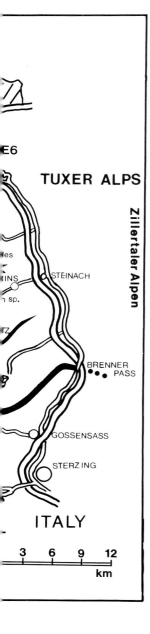

STUBAI ALPS HUTS

1 Dortmunder
2 Bielefelder
3 Gubener
4 Neue Pforzheimer
5 Potsdamer
6 Westfalenhaus
7 Winnebachsee
8 Franz Senn
9 Padasterjochhaus
10 Amberger
11 Neue Regensburger
12 Innsbrucker
13 Hochstubai
14 Dresdner
15 Sulzenau
16 Nürnberger
17 Bremer
18 Tribulaunhaus (Austr.)
19 Brunnenkogelhaus
20 Hildesheimer
21 Siegerland
22 Müller
23 Becherhaus
24 Teplitzer
25 Grohmann
26 Magdeburger
27 Tribulaun (Ital.)
28 Schneeberg

Introductory

GENERAL AND HISTORY

The Stubai Alps lie between the Zillertal Alps to the E and the
Ötztal Alps to the W. To the N they are contained by the Inn
valley, to the SE by the Jaufenpass road and SW by the Passeiertal and Timmelsjoch. The Austro-Ital. frontier ridge runs
roughly W from the Brenner Pass and turns S off the principal
mountain ridge (Hauptkamm) at the Wilder Pfaff. Forming the
main watershed the Hauptkamm continues W and NW to end by
Längenfeld in the Ötztal. The chief conurbation of the area is
Innsbruck, some 120 000 in population.

This is a rewarding region for mountaineers and walkers of all
standards. Many routes are in the lower grades of difficulty
and expeditions are often much shorter than in the Western Alps.
This gives an opportunity to adapt gradually and safely to more
arduous and technically demanding routes elsewhere. The highest
summits can be climbed by relatively straightforward glacier
routes which are usually well tracked in the season. Frequently
there are approaches from 2 or even 3 huts to the same mountain and this allows asecnts of peaks to be combined with interesting hut to hut transfers.

Whilst the easier snow routes enjoy by far the greatest popularity, a considerable number of harder climbs remain as well as
opportunities to explore remote peaks. The aim here is for a
broad selection of climbs with emphasis on mixed routes that
are typical of the area. Infinite good walking is also available
in the area. Apart from day trippers the most frequent users
of huts are walkers touring hut to hut. Therefore hut links
are fully described and include observations about problems
that can arise on mountain passes in order to assist in route
planning. High level transfers are generally easy and huts,
numbering more than 25, are rarely more than 6h apart and
usually less.

About 130 peaks top the 3000m mark, the highest being the
Zuckerhütl at 3505m. The largest glaciers are found on either
side of the Hauptkamm and in the Schrankogel-Ruderhofspitze-
Lisenser Fernerkogel group; they rarely give serious crevasse
problems by the normal routes. A few notable snow/ice faces
appear on Schrankogel, Habicht, Ruderhofspitze and the Östl.
Seespitze – but no long mixed climbs of great difficulty. In
the NW long rock ridges rise above deeply cut valleys and the
finest though remote peaks hereabouts such as the Strahlkogel
are seldom climbed.

Although geographically the **Kalkkögel** and **Kühtai Alps** are
part of the Stubai they may be regarded as separate specialist
areas for rock climbers and are not included in this volume.

*

It is probably fair to say that tourism in the Stubaital started in 1490 when the Emperor Maximilian I decided that it was a good place for holidays, albeit more for the hunting than the climbing. However Emperor Max is still often referred to as "The first German mountaineer". He wrote a book which included hints on climbing techniques and subsequently published details of a 6-pointed crampon. By the second half of the 18th century the Maria Waldrast monastery was attracting up to 40 000 visitors and pilgrims annually. The next influx, particularly in the period 1800-1840, was surprisingly of botanists, famous ones too, getting high into the mountains (even up to the snowline on Schrankogel) in their search for plants for specimen collecting and of course for medicines.

Then came the mountaineers. One name is prominent at the beginning of the era of mountain climbing by tourists in the Stubai. Professor Carl Thurwieser of Salzburg, born a miller's son in Kramsach in Tirol, had remarkable achievements to his name. In 1833 Strahlkogel was his first Stubai conquest though preceded by the Wildspitze and Similaun in the Ötztal earlier in the same year. In August 1836 he added the Lisenser Fernerkogel and Habicht which he called the Habichtspitze. His account of these latter climbs appeared in the house journal of the Ferdinandeum (Tyrolean State Museum in Innsbruck) in 1840. Since that day to this academics have played an important part in Alpinism throughout Austria. Indeed the first attempt at a climbing guide for the Stubai was published in 1865 by Professors Leopold Pfaundler and Ludwig Barth of Innsbruck just two years after they had stood on the Pfaffenschneide with their guide Alois Tanzer and sadly concluded that the peak to the E, the Zuckerhütl, was marginally higher. Confusingly they called Pfaffenschneid "Wilder Pfaff", the name now given to the peak lying immediately due E of Zuckerhütl.

The first ascent of Zuckerhütl came just a few days later by the taciturn though highly competent Viennese climber Specht with the same guide Tanzer. Ladies weren't idle either. On 20 September 1886 Therese Pfurtscheller from Fulpmes, with her brother and 2 guides, climbed Wilder Freiger, the Sonklarspitze, Wilder Pfaff and Zuckerhütl before walking down to Sölden for the night. On the following day they walked to the station at Ötztal (the Arlberg railway having opened in 1884), took the train to Innsbruck and walked back to Fulpmes. There is no relationship between this lady and the famous Ludwig Purtscheller, an early hard man, born in Innsbruck of a Stubai family and credited with many first ascents in our area as well as all over Europe and with the first ascent of Kilimanjaro.

The original English Stubai guide did not include detail of the South Tirol versant. This was largely because of the occupation of the huts by the Ital. Army and Customs authorities before and during the period of researching by Eric Roberts in the late 1960s. Moreover it was not unknown at that time for tourers crossing the frontier to be accosted by soldiers and, in the event of being unable to provide satisfactory proof of identity, flown to Bozen in a helicopter for interrogation. This made worthwhile routes on the Ital. side much longer and was unpopular with tourists for a long time. The events leading up to this situation and its ultimate resolution are germane to this brief historical survey.

The 1918 War Settlement Treaty of St Germain, in accordance with the secret 1915 Treaty of London which brought Italy into the war on the side of Britain and France, led to the annexation of the South Tirol to Italy – the then new border being the one existing today. It afforded the surest strategic security to Italy and indeed established Ital. rule for 400 000 or so Ital. speaking people.

However this part of the dismemberment of the Hapsburg Empire of Austro-Hungary also took 200 000 German-Austrians into Italy. As a result of this, from 1945 onwards, the South Tirol territorial dispute was one of the most troublesome problems that faced successive Austrian governments. An agreement on local autonomy for South Tirol was negotiated in 1946 between the respective Foreign Ministers but in Austrian eyes was never honoured. In the 1960s Austria brought the matter before the United Nations with no practically useful results. As historian Richard Rickett has written of that period: "The Foreign Ministers of Austria and Italy enjoyed conversations in many of Europe's most comfortable and picturesque resorts and issued cordial communiques thereafter".

During the same decade there were regular anti-Italian terrorist acts carried out by extremists in the South Tirol with no suggestion of political or cultural autonomy in sight. Eventually, between 1969 and 1971, culminating in the visit of the Austrian President Jonas to Italy, the dispute was settled amicably. Major political concessions to the German speaking peoples of the South Tirol were agreed and with concomitant relaxation of border tensions came the refurbishment and reopening of the Ital. Stubai club huts – though now of course under the auspices of the CAI. It is hugely regrettable that in 1988 there has been a resurgence of what can only be called terrorist bomb incidents in some South Tirol towns, fortunately thus far without loss of life.

ALPINE CLUBS

Membership of a UIAA affiliated alpine club offers considerable advantages, notably by way of a reduction in overnight fees in mountain huts (50% in many). However it should be noted that some huts owned by smaller organisations as opposed to those run by the ÖAV, DAV and CAI do not allow similar reductions. Many Austrophiles might prefer to join the ÖAV and there is an English section to cater for them. Address: Austrian Alpine Club (UK Branch), 13 Longcroft House, Fretherne Road, Welwyn Garden City, Herts. AL8 6PQ.

BERGSTEIGERBUROS (Guides' Offices)

The origins of local guides go back to the dawn of tourism in the valley itself and, amazingly, between 1869 and 1872 there was a formal agreement between the registered guides of a tariff of charges for the more popular routes. As elsewhere in the Alps the guides had "normal" occupations as well, commonly farming and hunting. In the early days many were not expert or experienced climbers themselves but had great toughness, enormous stamina and, most importantly, vast knowledge of local geography, likely dangers and a feel for weather. Many villages in the Stubai have a mountain guides office from where a wide range of types and grades of mountain activities are led (usually) by UIAA guides. Charges for the most frequented routes are prominently displayed. For other itineraries ask for a quote. Rates vary according to difficulty and numbers in a party - they will often be prepared to advertise for others to increase the group size and thus reduce cost to individuals. Be sure to ask about any additional costs, eg. for cableways/lifts, etc. and particularly about any charge arising in the event of cancellation because of bad weather or unexpected benightment in a mountain hut for example.

EQUIPMENT

It is assumed that users of this guide will be well versed in the basic and essential equipment required for alpine terrain. Rope, ice axe and crampons should be taken on most graded routes. Bivouac gear is rarely necessary though a survival bag is always worth space. On glacier routes prussik loops or other gadgets for crevasse rescue are recommended. Except on steep ice or serious rock routes with infamous stone fall danger the wearing of a helmet denotes a British climber. This must remain the choice of the individual.

Fixed ropes are found on certain popular peaks and on some hut connecting paths. They have long been considered by many to be an eyesore and an insult - Frank Smythe wrote rudely about their installation even in 1935. Whatever your prejudices on the matter beware of the relatively common frayed wire and loose fixtures on some of these cables.

MAPS AND GUIDEBOOKS

This work is written largely for use in conjunction with the AV maps on a scale 1/25 000. 2 maps cover most of the area, 31/1 Hochstubai (1984 ed.), 31/2 Sellrain (1981 ed.). The NE sector is covered by 31/5 Innsbruck Umgebung (1975) in 1/50 000, and includes the Serles-Habicht zone.

Note that notwithstanding the relatively recent publication dates the state of the glaciers is shown as at 1970 on 31/1 and as long ago as 1936-38 on 31/2. The eagle-eyed will spot discrepancies between the 2 sheets where they overlap, notably on the Bach-fallenferner. As these maps are available with either summer or ski route overprintings, be sure that you buy the map wanted.

No AV map is available at present for the Tribulaun group and much of the SE Ital. Stubai (originally 31/3). The official Öst-erreichische Karten (ÖK) are available in 1/25 000 for the whole of Austria. These are really only enlargements of the 1/50 000 versions. Though in some respects less detailed than AV maps, and often giving slightly different spot heights and spellings, they are nevertheless easy to read and useful for mountaineering. These are quoted in text for areas not covered by AV maps and only occasionally referred to otherwise. ÖK sheet nos. with their revision dates and, in brackets, dates at which the glaciers were last surveyed –

2705	146	Oetz	1975	(1975)	
2706	147	Axams	1982	(1970)	
2707	148	Brenner	1981	(1981)	
2710	174	Timmelsjoch	1982	(1970)	Ital. detail 1973
2711	175	Sterzing	1981	(1981)	Ital. detail 1970

Official Ital. mapping (IGM) is military restricted and not in the public domain. However, IGM 1/25 000 issues right across the South Tirol zone have been consulted for writing the guide.

Extensive commercial mapping of a good standard, all with tourist information overprints, is published across the Stubai Alps and covers the Ital. side as follows in 1/50 000 (50M) with one in 1/100 000 (100M) – all sheets overlap considerably –

FB series	24	100M	Stubaier Alpen
	241	50M	Stubai-Sellrain
	251		Ötztal-Pitztal
	S4		Sterzing-Brixen
	S8		Passeier-Timmelsjoch
KK series	36	50M	Innsbruck-Brenner
	43		Ötztaler Alpen
	44		Sterzing
	83		Stubaier Alpen

All maps cited above are sold in the UK by West Col Productions.

The German language guide for the area **Stubaier Alpen** by Heinrich and Walter Klier is a helpful source of information on less frequented routes. Many more rock climbs are to be found in the Klier guide. A new edition was published at the end of 1988 and it can be bought in most of the major Stubai villages. As in many volumes of this AVF guide series, a shorter version is published additionally, aimed at selecting from the easier walks and climbs. Several other German and Italian works also exist.

Noted in 1989, current reprinting of AV maps leaves a lot to be desired in resulting clarity which suffers badly from dark inking.

ALTITUDES - ORIENTATION - NOMENCLATURE

Most altitudes are taken from AV maps. Where an altitude is not shown it has been calculated from contour lines and/or measured with an altimeter. Some detailed information on the Ital. (S) side of the frontier has been ascertained from IGM mapping which as noted above is military restricted. Heights and vertical intervals are expressed in metres.

Where there exists a commonly used alternative name for a pass, mountain or hut it is indicated in text. German language terms eg. "ferner" for glacier have been largely (but not always) retained. Also, S of the frontier German names have been adopted where appropriate purely for cartographical and historical reasons as well as continuity. Though Ital. territory, no political inference is intended.

The directions "left" (L) and "right" (R) have been applied entirely in the sense of direction of movement of the climber. Compass directions may also be given to assist route finding.

ROUTE GRADINGS

The conventional 6 categories represented by their initial letters are used to denote the grades of general mountaineering routes on mixed terrain (see below). This indicates overall seriousness and is affected by several factors including length of climb, technical difficulties, how sustained, objective dangers, etc. In addition, on routes where significant rock climbing is involved, the difficulty of the hardest pitch is graded numerically in accordance with the UIAA system. Sometimes a note to indicate whether this is sustained is added. Less experienced climbers should remember that mountains in the Stubai are smaller and the routes shorter than in the Western Alps, and this can create the danger of a false sense of values. A glacier route of Facile (F) standard in the W.Alps might involve far more serious problems than its equivalent in the Stubai. It is also prudent to note that Facile is a relative term in this context and should never be taken literally as "Easy". It should be borne in mind that prevailing weather conditions may affect grading considerably. An extensively snow filled cirque in early July might well be perfectly dreadful as a boulderfield by mid August. A note on the grading of hut approaches or connections appears in the Huts section. Remember, there is always a degree of subjective judgement in the allocation of grades of difficulty to a route as well as changes in environmental detail.

F-   Walking routes on paths with some rough or steep ground. Easy trackless terrain, snow but no crevassed glaciers.

F   Facile. Steep walking, rock scrambling and easy snow slopes. Crevasses possible on glaciers.

F+   Sustained rock scrambling. Crevassed glaciers.

PD-	Rock climbing though short pitches only. Steep snow slopes.
PD	Peu difficile. Rock climbing with some technical difficulty. Snow and ice slopes, narrow ridges, difficult glaciers.
PD+	Sustained rock climbing. Steep snow/ice slopes.
AD-	Short hard rock pitches, short snow/ice faces.
AD	Assez difficile. Fairly difficult and serious climbs. Steep rock climbing. Long snow/ice slopes above 50°.
AD+	As above with occasionally harder and more delicate bits.
D-	Hard rock and snow/ice climbing.
D	Difficile. As above and sustained.
D+	As D but with more technical pitches.
TD	Très difficile. Very difficult technical climbing on all kinds of terrain
ED	Extrêmement difficile. Extremely serious climbs with sustained difficulties of the highest order. XD Exceptionally difficult - has been added to this scale in recent years.

UIAA rock climbing grades

The scale of difficulty is revised from time to time. A 1988 revision contains attempts to cope with ever rising standards of "free climbing". An older scale is described here with the approximate traditional British equivalents. High and low in grade are denoted by plus and minus signs. It should be remembered that this is very subjective particularly in the lower grades.

I	Minor difficulties, at most only mild scrambling.
II	Scrambling. A rope may be important for many.
III	Moderate. Many experienced climbers would not use rope.
III+	Difficult. IV Very Difficult. V Severe.
V+	Hard Severe (about 4b).
VI-	Very Severe (about 4c). VI Hard Very Severe (5a)
VI/VII-	E1. VII E2. VIII- E3. VIII E4.
VIII+/IX-	E5. IX E6/7.

MOUNTAIN RESCUE

In the event of an accident or incident, the hut warden (Hüttenwirt) or local police are the best points of contact. In 1988 Mountain Rescue services in Austria were free of charge to members of ÖAV and certain affiliated organisations as well as

those in possession of local "Guest Cards". However it is prudent to have adequate Insurance and essential if contemplating
straying over the Ital. frontier.
The standard Alpine emergency signal is 6 whistle blasts or
torch flashes within one minute, regularly spaced. This is followed by a one minute pause and repeated as required. The
reply is 3 whistles or flashes also within a minute.

WEATHER REPORTS

Austrian TV/Radio weather reports are neither sufficiently detailed nor reliable enough for mountaineering purposes. However
Austrian Radio Channel 3 does give these reports (Wetterlage -
literally weather conditions) at the end of the News on the hour
virtually all day. A better local forecast can be obtained by
ringing Innsbruck Weather Centre (05222-1567) for a 24 hour
recorded message: or 05222-21839 between 13.00 and 18.00 h
daily for a direct conversation with one of the staff. No weather information of any kind is presently available at local
Tourist Offices - an important oversight which should be rem-
edied by the authorities.

TIMINGS

All numbered routes and hut approaches/connections have time
estimates included as a rough guide. They represent the time
taken excluding stops for an average party with average pack
and gear, rather than that of a solitary fell runner in T-shirt
and Y-fronts. When routes are done in the reverse direction
from that described, then an approx. adjustment will need to be
made.

ROUTE NUMBERING

Route numbers are prefixed R. where they occur in the body
of the text. Do not confuse with official path numbers seen on
maps. The latter are not generally cited in text to avoid con-
fusion. Usually official numbered paths are well waymarked,
and the number may be painted on rocks or noted on signposts.
On the AV Hochstubai map path numbers are not included for
the Ital. side of the frontier. In view of this some path nos.
in this particular area are cited in the guide, eg. Path No.

GLOSSARY

Most terms used are in such frequent use among the British
that no further explanation is required. Some that may be
less familiar to those with little command of German are -

Alm	Mountain pasture, usually with chalets
Bach	Stream
Ferner	Glacier
Grube	Hollow, basin

Hang	Slope
Hütte	Hut - in sense of one used by climbers, etc.
Joch(Jöchl)	Pass, col (diminutive form)
Kar	Cirque
Nieder	Gap, low point on ridge, small col
Rinne	Gully, couloir
Scharte	Notch, gap in ridge, saddle - interchangeable with Nieder
See	Lake
Tal	Valley
Weg	Path

ACKNOWLEDGEMENTS

Many people have helped and advised during the preparation of this guide and it would be impossible to name all individually. Special thanks are due to climbing colleagues for companionship, reports and often great patience. In alphabetical order - David Allan (also the cartoonist), Chris Davies, Rob Pealing, Carl Pierce, Helen & Steve Swygart, John Williams and Tina & Gareth Williams.

Luis Töchterle of the ÖAV has been not only a friend and climbing companion but also a major source of local information. In particular he is to be thanked for allowing me access to the OAV Library Archives and for introductions to local guides and climbers. Wolfgang Theyssen, a dear friend and colleague, unearthed much background detail and provided photographic advice.

My wife Maryann and children Kate and Jeremy showed enormous forbearance during their total Stubai immersion of the last few years though we all have huge affection for the area. They have walked/climbed a large number of the routes described in the book.

And of course without Eric Roberts' original work there wouldn't be a successor. It is to his memory that this work is dedicated.

PUBLISHERS' NOTE

In common with all volumes in this series, the majority of itineraries described by the author has been accomplished either by himself or by parties associated with the same comprehensive survey of the region. In the best traditions commenced by Eric Roberts in various parts of the Austrian Tirol, there is no secondhand or translated material in this volume, and errors arising are merely those of human slipups associated with computerisation of the record for the Stubai. Work is in hand for updating other regions of Austria to the same high standards.

Approaches

The best train service runs from Calais via Basel, Zürich, to Buchs and the Voralberg, leaving London early afternoon and arriving Innsbruck in the middle of the following morning. It stops at Ötztal, the station sited in the Inntal at junction of the 2 valleys, whence a bus goes up the Ötztal to Sölden, etc.

Air travel is increasingly popular and at present there is a direct service from Gatwick to Innsbruck with APEX fares little different from train fares – especially if couchette or sleeper costs are counted. An alternative routing is via Zürich with a local airline onwards.

By road to Innsbruck is virtually equidistant (about 1090 km) from Vlissingen (from Sheerness), Hook of Holland (from Harwich) and Ostend (from Dover). The latter routes offer Autobahn driving from the port right to the entrance of the Stubaital off the Brenner Pass section of motorway. The other route entails only a few km of non-motorway driving and the choice of sea-crossing is dictated therefore primarily by ease of access from home to port of embarkation. Note that there is a toll for using the motorway between Innsbruck and Brenner on the Ital. border. This can be avoided by taking the old Brenner pass road (No.182), though longer and winding. If several trips along the motorway look likely, even just between the Stubaital and Innsbruck, then a month season ticket is a bargain at about 4 times the price of one return ticket.

There are direct bus services from Innsbruck up the Stubai valley, Sellraintal, Ötztal and Wipptal (for Gschnitztal, the Eastern section of the Hauptkamm, Tribulaun group, etc.). Also a frequent local train service through the Wipptal and across the Ital. frontier. The narrow gauge electric Stubaitalbahn from outside Innsbruck main station (Hauptbahnhof) to Fulpmes, constructed in 1904 largely to serve the steel industry, is of little use unless you are based in Fulpmes itself. Timetables of these services and other local information especially about the superb Museums and churches which abound in Innsbruck, can be obtained from the Tourist office (Fremdenverkehrsverband) at Burggraben 3 (Tel: 25715). On a wet or rest day the Alpine Museum and the Zeughaus, the latter noted for geological detail and a history of avalanche origins and defences, can be especially recommended to all.

Valley Bases

The choice of a single base for climbing or walking is governed largely by the preferred area for exploration. The Stubaital and Neustift in particular is probably the best centre for the most interesting climbs and access to a variety of huts for touring. Notes are included about facilities available at a selection of villages for consideration as bases, and points of re-supply or a provider of creature comforts. The term "accommodation" embraces a range of possibilities from grand hotels to the meanest bed-and-breakfast establishment. Special note should be made of public holidays to avoid disappointment, starvation and penury. The banks vary considerably in their opening times and almost always close for anything up to 3 h at lunchtime.

STUBAITAL

From which the Stubai Alps takes its name. A beautiful valley extending SW from Schönberg. Regular bus service from Innsbruck starting from the bus station - some 100m L as you leave the Hauptbahnhof.

Fulpmes is the large village in the valley, with 3000 inhabitants more a small town. At 935m the nearest place in the valley to Innsbruck to merit consideration as a base. Supermarkets, hotels, chalets, a thriving guides' office and of course the well known Stubai climbing equipment cooperative. Terminus of the Stubaitalbahn which starts, tram-like, just outside the Hauptbahnhof. As a centre Fulpmes is probably just a bit removed from the action though with a car this would be unimportant.

Neustift at 993m and about 30 km from Innsbruck is quite a small village but with supermarkets, lots of accommodation, several banks and the last post office. Several smaller collections of houses, hotels, etc. use Neustift as a prefix, eg. Neustift-Kampl, Neustift-Neder and so on. Campsite with good facilities right by the main square and good indoor and outdoor swimming pools. Probably the best centre in the area. Further up the valley the villages and hamlets become progressively smaller though all have accommodation. A campsite and shop at Volderau, wrecked completely in the 1987 floods, are now rebuilt and said to be safer. Mutterbergalm has only hotels and a kiosk.

GSCHNITZTAL

Leading SW off the Wipptal at Steinach am Brenner which is the railhead. Bus service up the valley from here to Feuerstein. Plentiful accommodation right up the valley though concentrated at **Trins** and **Gschnitz** (for the Tribulaun, Bremer and Innsbrucker huts). Both these villages have banks, shops and a

post office and Trins has a tourist office. No official campsites.
It is worthwhile approaching local landowners or hoteliers for
permission to camp discretely on their land. Permission is
often granted and obviates awkward moments. This applies to
all places without regular sites.

SELLRAINTAL

This pretty valley, not much frequented by tourists in summer,
branches SW off the Inntal at Kematen 12 km W of Innsbruck.
The villages from E to W are **Sellrain** (909m, for Potsdamer hut),
Gries (1190m, for the Lisensertal and Westfalenhaus), **Sankt
Sigmund** (1516m, for Neue Pforzheimer hut), **Haggen** (1650m)
and **Kühtai** (1976m). All have accommodation though the hotels
in Kühtai are quite expensive and, being largely a winter
sports resort, something of a ghost town in summer. All except
Haggen have a shop or two; Kühtai has a bank. No official
campsites. A bus service operates from Innsbruck right through
the valley.

ÖTZTAL

Extends generally S from Ötztal Bahnhof, the station on the
Innsbruck-Arlberg line, to Sölden, the largest village and last
useful base in the valley for the Stubai. Bus services from
Innsbruck and from Ötztal Bahnhof, right down the valley.
Although several villages in the main valley or in the eastern
side valleys provide a jumping-off pt. for a hut approach or
two, none can be said to be really satisfactory bases.

Oetz (820m), the road junction for the western end of the Sellraintal, has shops, banks and a campsite as well as being attr-
actively situated below the Neue Bielefelder hut and the boldly
impressive Acherkogel.

Umhausen (1031m) is similar. To enter the mountains one must
take the E-side valley road (minibus) up to **Niederthai** (1535m),
accommodation and a shop. This is the start for the valley
approach to the Gubener-Schweinfurt hut. A better option is
Gries im Sulztal, the valley E of Längenfeld; it has a bus service, good prospects for accommodation and a couple of shops
but no campsite. More alpine atmosphere here than its Ötztal
neighbours and is usefully placed for good walks including the
approaches to the Amberger and Winnebachsee huts.

Sölden (1352m) has everything: hotels, chalets, shops, pools,
campsite, guides' office - everything that is except atmosphere.
It is a long walk to any of the huts, and more properly serves
the Ötztal Alps region.

PFLERSCHTAL

Ital. Val di Fleres. The first of the Ital. valleys after crossing the border at Brenner. The railhead is at Gossensass

(Ital. Colle Isarco) on the main Innsbruck-Italy railway. Bus service up the valley from here for 8 km to **Innerpflersch**, also known as St Anton in Pflersch and St Antonio (1246m). This is the road end proper. Small shop, a few hotels and other accommodation; no bank, no campsite. The Ital. Tribulaun and Magdeburger huts can be approached from here.

RIDNAUNTAL

Ital. Val di Ridanna. The only other properly useful valley for the Ital. side of the region. Starting pt. for approaches to the Teplitzer and Becher huts. Railhead at Sterzing (Ital. Vipiteno) on the main railway as above. From here bus service up the valley to roadhead just past **Maiern** (1426m) with a small shop and limited accommodation. **Ridnaun** itself (1342m) has only accommodation but **Mareit** lower down the valley has shops and a post office. Lone campsite in a dismal wood at Gasteig, the junction of the valley road and the Jaufenpass road. A bank is at **Stange**, the small village at junction of the Ridnauntal and the Ratschingstal.

PASSEIERTAL

Ital. Val di Passiria. Included for completeness. One can enter the Stubai Alps from here via the Schneeberg hut or of course over the Timmelsjoch road. **Moos in Passeier** is a pleasant village with shops and a bank. Bus service from St Leonhard lower down the valley through Moos to Sölden.

Huts

The extensive network of huts serving the Stubai has its origins over 100 years ago with the opening of the Dresdner hut in 1875 and followed quickly by the Innsbrucker (1884) and the Franz Senn (1885). Most are now owned by national alpine clubs. The popular ones have been enlarged or modernised in the last 20 years and are comfortable with adequate facilities - usually only cold running water though a few huts have warm water and showers. Some remote huts remain more primitive and may retain a curious original charm. Certain high huts have no water on tap at all. Electric or gas lighting is commonly available but may only be supplied to certain rooms. A small torch is useful.

Accommodation is mainly in dormitories (Matratzenlager - abbreviated "Lager"), consisting of long communal beds or bunks with blankets and pillows supplied. For a higher charge there are also bunks/beds with linen/duvets in rooms for 1-6 people. A sheet sleeping bag is a good idea for dormitories.

Advance booking by ÖAV members is permitted in some huts but no-one is ever turned away - at times of overcrowding extra places are created by putting mattresses on the floor. In complete contrast to France and certain parts of the Western Alps this is unusual in the Stubai. Depending on the demand for places you may not be allowed to stay for more than 3 consecutive nights.

Meals are relatively expensive, especially breakfast. All huts are obliged to provide a meal of specific weight (500g - called Bergsteigeressen); this is filling but of unpredictable quality and often contains little or no meat. Otherwise there is a choice of food, sometimes of excellent quality, albeit at a price. You may take and eat your own food but there are no self-catering facilities. Gas or other types of stove cannot be used in the huts. Most wardens (Hüttenwirt or Pächter, the latter literally tenant) will not have the time or inclination to cook visitors' food as is done in some other countries. Beer, wine, soft drinks, coffee, etc. can be purchased but are also expensive. It is common practice to buy hot water (Teewasser) and prepare one's own beverages. Therefore "the makings" are worth carrying up and many take enough food to provide at least a breakfast and snacks.

If a very early start is contemplated, and there is space in the 'sac, a thermos (for Teewasser collected the night before) or a stove (to use outside in the morning) would be useful. Because of the brevity of many routes few parties start in the dark and the practice is discouraged by hut wardens. The notable exceptions to this habit are the British who are widely considered eccentric on the subject.

Most hut walks are easy but connections may not be. If no grade is given this infers that it is suitable for competent walkers without special equipment unless there is a note to the contrary. Nevertheless ground conditions can change quickly in adverse weather and a normally straightforward pass could present serious problems for the unprepared or inexperienced.

The Hüttenwirt is often a helpful source of information on routes and local conditions. Some hut walks are long; the most tiresome is the slog up from Sölden to the Siegerland. Many huts transport provisions, etc. by cable hoist - in the vernacular = Materialseilbahn. It is often possible to send your rucksack up for a moderate charge. Visitors are never allowed to ride on these contraptions.

Most huts have a telephone. Sometimes it may be helpful to call the warden if information on specific points or a query about booking are required. Remember that many wardens do not speak English.

Austrian huts do not usually provide hut shoes though invariably forbid the wearing of boots in dormitories and bedrooms. Moccasins/slippers may be worthwhile. A master key for unattended huts or huts out of season is available from the ÖAV for a small charge. In these instances there may be access to only part of the hut (Winterraum) or even to a separate small building nearby (Notlager - literally emergency room). Unattended huts normally have blankets, firewood and rescue equipment, but no provisions. Out of the "advertised season" for a particular hut it is prudent to check on accessibility before setting out.

Payment at huts is virtually always in cash; rarely, Eurochecks may be accepted. Generally it is preferred and advantageous to pay in local currency - Austrian Schillings or Italian Lire as appropriate. Most DAV huts will also accept German Marks and the South Tirol (Ital.) huts always take Schillings as an acceptable alternative to Lire. Whether the rate of exchange is acceptable to the customer is another matter.

AMBERGER   2135m

DAV Sekt Amberg. Situated at E foot of the Niederer Sulzkogel where the upper Sulztal opens out into a basin. There is a small lake (Schmefelsee) containing respectably-sized trout just below the hut with a warm spring as part-source.

b.1888, enl.1937/38, 1975/76. Tel: 05253-5605. Open: mid June - end September. B 18, M 75. Parking: Gries im Sulztal. PT. Gries (bus).

1   From obvious carpark at the E end of **Gries** village follow clear track SE up the Sulztal, passing the Vord. Sulztalalm before turning S through a narrow section of the valley immediately before reaching hut (2h).

Can we have the car keys before you do the next bit.

2   From **Dresdner** hut go W to where the Neue Regensburger hut path branches off R and descend slightly to cross stream before climbing the opposite bank steeply in zigzags. The next bit is dreadful - see also R.33a; bulldozed boulders and mud created by landscaping apparently required for satisfactory ski-ing here are particularly unpleasant when snow cover has rec-ently melted.   Cross the stream again wherever you can, aiming to pass N of the large (and in summertime) deserted restaurant facility, thence onto the Daunkogelferner, regaining alpine sights and sanity.   Continue WNW up the enclosed snow/boulder slope to the Daunjoch (3057m) where there is a small lake; an excellent view of Wilde Leck.   Descend moderately steep snow onto the Sulztalferner.   From this pt. the indicated route on the 1984 AV map is misleading, taking one into territory of gully and stonefall. There are 2 viable options:

(a)   In late season and/or poor visibility in this direction of travel it is easier to contour the glacier at c2980m to intersect with the Wütenkarsattel-Amberger hut route (R.32) on W side of the glacier, F.

(b)   For the more adventurous go NW from foot of the Daunjoch slope to tip of the rocky promontory just below 2800m and go dpwn N, parallel to the rocks before crossing the glacier NW where it flattens out to the moraine edge at c2500m, and take the waymarked path which curves NW round rocks to join R.32 at c2280m.   About 20 min. from there to hut, PD-.   About 4-5h by either route.

Done in the opposite direction, the latter way is more attractive, particularly as the condition of the steepest part of the glacier can be ascertained earlier.   Note that the Daunjoch may be hard to find from the Sulztalferner side in poor visibility and is not marked on the rocks at the base.

3   From **Franz Senn** hut follow the marked path SW on R of the stream.   Little height is gained for 30 min., then at 2300m the path steepens just after crossing the Berglas stream, sub-sequently taking the R(W) bank moraine of the Alpeinerferner, passing pt.2616.   The path finishes at c2750m.   Head up W side of the glacier, keeping the icefall on the L and passing foot of the N. Wildgratspitze E ridge.   Then move W to the Wildgratscharte (3168m), 3-3h30.   On W side of the col descend a short scree/snow slope to upper basin of the Schwarzenberg-ferner and contour SW (crevasses) to reach the E ridge of the Schrankogel at c3100m.   Continue down W side of the moraine, finally curving NW and N over grass down into the Sulztal and crossing stream just by the hut, F+.   About 5h30.

Note: The Schwarzenbergjoch, just S of the Südl. Wildgratspitze, is almost never used as a summer connection between the Sch-warzenbergferner and the Alpeinerferner except for occasional Amberger to Ruderhofspitze parties.

4   From the **Westfalenhaus** go generally S above and W of the Längentaler Bach without gaining much height for 40 min. or so to a signpost at c2420m where the Hoher Seeblaskogel path breaks R. Subsequently the way leads up the moraine bank steeply before crossing the valley to ascend E side of the Längentalferner, following edge of the glacier (crevasses) to the Längentaljoch (2991m), 2h30. The descent through the Schrankar is straightforward, SSE to join and reverse R.62 at the signpost c2720m. About 5h hut to hut, F.

Hut connections: **Hochstubai**, R.32. **Winnebachsee**, R.62.

BECHERHAUS   3190m

CAI Sekt Verona. Now as Rif. Gino Biasi al Bicchiere, though originally the Kaiserin Elisabeth Haus when, before World War I it belonged to the Austro-German Alpine Club's Hanover section. At one stage also called Königin Elana Haus and Rif. Regina Elena – all very confusing. The highest hut in the Stubai Alps and perched spectacularly on the Becher rocks in the Übeltalferner. Seen from the direction of the Teplitzer hut, particularly if partially cloaked in mist, eerily reminiscent of a medieval castle. Extensive refurbishment was taking place in 1988.

b.1893. Radio telephone. Open: beginning July–mid September. B 90, M 90. Parking/public transport – see Grohmann hut. No running water.

5   The route from the **Ridnauntal** starts at the disused iron ore extraction plant just above Maiern. Though a long walk it is a generally pleasant and interesting approach with formal imbibing halts possible at Grohmann and Teplitzer huts en route. (In 1988 the Grohmann was again closed when visited; it would be prudent not to rely on this facility).
After indifferent start amidst old mining buildings, the waymarked path (No.9) goes steeply up the L side of a gorge then follows the stream closely to a large alp/plateau (Agglsboden) at c1700m where there is a small dam which carries the path to R side of the valley. The hut seen on the skyline from here is the Teplitzer, a potentially morale-lowering sight which should be statutorily forbidden. Steep zigzags follow over a rocky step to c2000m (note pleasant picnic site by a waterfall c1980m). Here the valley narrows again. Having surmounted the step the path after a flattish section mounts gradually up the R hillside to the tiny Grohmann hut, sited on a rocky outcrop and coming into view soon after passing 2000m (2h30). A short but steep track winds up through boulders NW then N without difficulty to the Teplitzer hut in 45 min. (Note that on both AV map and ÖK 2710 a small path is marked bypassing the Teplitzer hut, leaving the track at c2420m and rejoining it above the Teplitzer just E of the lake at 2620m. In 1987 this path was dangerous and is better avoided). After the Teplitzer continue W, crossing the stream which runs down from the Hangender Ferner, and wind round the hillside eventually passing N of an obvious glacier lake. In a short way the path turns NNW along a moraine bank and through boulders before crossing the glacier W to foot of Becher rocks. Almost 400m still remains over steep rocks with several

short exposed gangway sections protected by (1987) good fixed plastic cables (3-3h30; allow 6-7h from Maiern excluding stops).

6　From **Müller** hut start out W but drop immediately down rocks to the Übeltalferner and head roughly E towards the Becher rocks and hut. Small diversions often necessary to turn crevasses but in 40 min. reach pt.3157, the small saddle N of hut. Thence up a wooden staircase to the stone steps and a Roman road-like construction in a few min. F+.

7　From **Magdeburger** hut follow R.53 over the Magdeburger Scharte, passing N of obvious rock island on W side of the pass. Then keep to N side of the Hangender Ferner below Weites and Enges Türl onto the small Geisswandferner, over the Rotgratscharte to the Freigerscharte. Below and W of this contour high round the glacier to saddle pt.3157 and continue as for R.6 (5-6h), PD. In poor visibility there may be route finding problems, particularly on the Feuersteiner Ferner – see R.53. (Clearly an alternative would be to go to the Teplitzer hut and combine R.53 with R.5).

8　From **Nürnberger** or **Sulzenau** huts adopt R.85 as far as the Signalgipfel. Then descent easy rocks S down to the glacier and continue S to pt.3157; now follow R.6. One could also go to the Wilder Freiger summit, down the snow slope onto the Übeltalferner just W of the peak, then follow the glacier round to the same pt.3157 as above (4h30), F.

Hut connection: **Schneeberg**, R.49.

BIELEFELDER　　2112m

DAV Sekt Bielefeld. Sited on a promontory W of the Rossköpfe with nice views over the Ötztaler Alps and W into the Inntal. Unfortunately, just off W edge of the AV map.

b.1953/54, enl.1986 – replacing old hut destroyed by avalanche, see R.11 – new hut is really **Neue** Bielefelder hut. Tel: 05252-6650. Open: mid-June to end September. B 35, M 36. Parking: Kühtaier Alm or Oetz. PT. Oetz (bus). The Acherkogelbahn (2-stage, 2-seater chairlift) top station, Bergrestaurant Hochoetz (2020m) is only 30 min. from hut.

9　A long trek up from **Oetz** and involves an ascent of some 1300m, taking about 4h. The hut can be seen from the village. If this hasn't persuaded you towards the chairlift read on. Of a number of variations to the walk it is probably best to start by the open-air swimming pool at S end of the village. The route is poorly signed before this and easiest access is via a small path starting immediately L of chairlift station (more temptation). Initially go parallel with the valley road then turn E through woods and occasional meadows pleasantly all the way.

After the start it is generally well signed and waymarked; a
forestry road appears from time to time which is unmarked on
some maps. After passing Acherbergalm head N up a rocky tree
clad step to hut.
An alternative is to walk up from road at Unterhäusen/Ochsen-
garten. The path goes steeply SSE through woods to Balbach-
Sennhütte (1955m). The upper of two possible paths goes W
round the shoulder of the Rossköpfe and turn S to the Bielefelder hut (2h); not all that interesting but much shorter on
foot than from Oetz.

10   From **Dortmunder** hut go down the Oetz road to where the
road recrosses the river to its L bank at an area called Alte
Klause. A track goes back SE initially but climbs the hillside
generally W to the Oberer Issalm (1929m). Next up the Wör-
getal SSW, turning WNW up to the Wetterkreuz (2578m), a small
top directly above the hut. Then go W down a marked path
via the Rossköpfe (2399m) to join R.11 about 10 min. above and
E of the hut (4h).

An attractive option lies up the Mittertal, starting at the SW
corner of the Speicher Längental dam lake. This leads to the
easy Mittertalscharte at pt.2630. Then either go down the
marked path, initially scree, towards the Old hut using R.161
or, more sportingly, do the ridge running N from the col,
rounding the Gr. and Kl. Windegg on their W flank to the
Wetterkreuz or without difficulty over the summits.

11   Leave the **Gubener** hut N down the wide track and across
a stream bridge before taking small signed path for the Hochreichscharte. Almost immediately note a path going NE towards
the Finstertalerscharte and Kühtai. Our path runs up the valley just N of W, staying on N bank of stream and past the huts
on Finstertal Alp with a spectacular view of Strahlkogel to the S.
The direction is more or less straight towards the easy Steinkar
Ferner, traversed to its N edge and up to the Hochreichscharte
(2912m). The last bit is steep, scree and often snow, some red
waymarks and even a couple of abseil pegs for no very obvious
reason - perhaps there is ice late in the season (3h so far).

The normal route then descends steeply over loose stones, turning the Hochreichkopf on its W side before mounting to meet the
NW ridge of the same mountain at c2890m, and descending steeply
to the Niederreichscharte (2728m). The easy path down the Längental towards Kühtai and the Dortmunder hut branches NE here
- a useful escape route in deteriorating weather conditions; for
detail see R.163.
Many would prefer to traverse the Hochreichkopf instead of turning it - straightforward and just as quick - see R.165,166.
Now descend a little NW across the flank of the Hochbrunnach-
kogel to "Am Lauser" (cairn) where the marked path turns down
steeply N into the stony Acherkar; often large snow patches. To
the NE the Gr. Wechnerkogel looks particularly impressive. The

next bit seems endless, round corners, across gullies often full
of snow to early July, down fixed ropes, all the while gradually
gaining height to emerge on crest of the Acherkogel W ridge at
Achplatte (2423m), just off the AV map though shown on ÖK 2705.
Next very steeply indeed down in zigzags, turning NE to level
ground at site of the Old hut destroyed in 1951. From here the
new hut is visible NW on a promontory. The well signed path
now rises gradually N and after crossing a series of gullies
finally turns W and down to hut. Note en route from Old hut
a path L down to Acherbergalm and Oetz and 2 paths R. The
first leaves almost immediately from hut site itself up towards the
Mittertalscharte; the second trending up NE to the Wetterkreuz.

The usually quoted time for this route is 6-7h, but with poor
weather, snow in the gullies or even just a heavy pack, 8h is a
good time. Local informants suggest that many parties take a
lot longer. The route is not to be underestimated and earns its
F grading even though under normal circumstances there is little
objective danger and no technical climbing.

BREMER   2413m

Beautifully situated on the Mitteregg at foot of the Innere Wetterspitze E ridge. Can be very busy; a popular attraction is
the triangular excursion of Gschnitz - Bremer hut - Innsbrucker hut - Gschnitz, often including Habicht. DAV Sekt Bremen.

b.1897. Tel: 0663-57545. Open: all July - mid September.
B 22, M 36. Parking: Gschnitz Feuerstein. PT. as parking
(bus). Cable hoist: Laponesalm - telephone the hut.

12   From **Gschnitz** follow road SW up the valley to Laponesalm
(1480m), restaurant. Note that private vehicles are not allowed
further than the Feuerstein Inn at Gschnitz - Obertal. After
Laponesalm, a short way up the valley the track zigzags steeply
W up slopes on the N side. Reach a pleasant plateau at c2000m
by the middle station of the cable hoist. (Another path comes
up S of the Gschnitzbach to meet here but it is an unattractive
option). Now continue S then W on a well marked path to hut
(3h from Laponesalm).

13   The way from the **Innsbrucker** hut is a waymarked and
much frequented route with rewarding views in good weather.
In snow it can be exceptionally difficult to find the path; it is
well graded but crosses several ridges and their associated
valleys as it winds SW. A few fixed ropes are often unnecesu-
sary and unreliable; several waterfalls and an abundance of
picnic sites.
Soon after crossing the Äussere Wetterspitze E ridge the old
track to the Bremer hut forks R. This is now difficult to find
and is not signposted; after it passes just below the Lauterer
See it becomes easier to follow and includes a steep ascent of
slabs with (1987) good fixed cables. It is presumably because

of this unexpected excitement that the recommended path makes a diversion across the Simmingalpe further E to join the ascent route from Gschnitz just before the hut (5h). The older route is no longer marked on AV map.

14   From **Nürnberger** hut go SE over slabby rocks, passing the signpost R for the Wilder Freiger route, and down quite steeply to cross the Langenbach. Now head NE, later E, to follow path in an arc up close to S flank of the Inn. Wetterspitze and over a scree/snowfield. Finally rise steeply S to the Simmingjöchl (2764m); old customs hut now refurbished for a reason unknown. Now steeply with care down a scree gully E; this has deteriorated considerably in the last few years and there is stonefall danger. Then descend easily NE to the hut (3h30).

Hut connection: **Magdeburger**. The Bremer Scharte, also known as the Nördl. Stuben Scharte, is a difficult crossing; it is easier to traverse the Schneespitz, R.94,92.

BRUNNENKOGELHAUS   2735m

OTK Wien. Small old hut on the Vord. Brunnenkogel, really only useful for a traverse of the Windachkamm. As a walk the round trip described below is most enjoyable and with excellent views.

b.1887 (ÖTC Sekt Otztal), enl.1903 (ÖTK Sekt Wien). No telephone. Open: early June - mid September. B 2, M 13. Parking: Sölden. PT. Sölden.

15   From **Sölden** walk S on L bank of the Ötztaler Ache river and cross the Windache stream. Immediately after the bridge a signposted path goes L steeply and pleasantly in woods. At c1450m take the R fork (L for the Windachtal). Subsequently cross paths and tracks but the way is always signed or red/white marked. At c1710m is the "Brunnenberg-Stabele Alm-Jausenstation Falkner". Look carefully for the very small signed path behind the buildings, heading generally NE up to Falkner Wirtshaus proper (1972m). Now the path goes SE, soon over open hillside and later gaining height only slowly until suddenly turning NE and zigzagging steeply to hut (3h30-4h).

A recommended round trip is continued by leaving the hut SE on a path and immediately zagging down into a stony basin NE, and climbing slightly to cross the NE ridge of the Hint. Brunnenkogel. Now in the wide and aptly-named Schönkar, traverse to its E side and finally steeply N down along a small stream. At a T-junction turn R(E), contouring into the next valley, then turn N and wind pleasantly down through woods to the Windache stream some 300m E of Fiegl's Gasthaus. Easy path all the way, better done in the direction described; lovely views; the impressive peak seen ENE from the hut is Pfaffenschneid (1h30-2h to Fiegl's). Then reverse R.26, about 1h30 down to Sölden.

DORTMUNDER   1948m

DAV Sekt Dortmund. At the W end of Kühtai. Easy of access,
with hot showers and much more hotel-like than most huts.

b.1931/32. Tel: 05239-202. Open: all June – end October.
B 36, M 38. Parking: Kühtai. PT. Kühtai (bus).

16   From **Gubener** hut start on a path N. Soon take R fork
and ascend grass slopes NE into a broad cirque (Weites Kar).
Continue N and scramble NW up scree/snow to the Finstertaler
Scharte (2719m). The path descends more scree slopes on N
side, often with snow patches, curving W at c2520m round the
Finstertaler Fernerkogel NE spur to join R.167 at c2380m. So
reverse this to hut, F- (4h).
Note: When undertaking traverse in the opposite direction the
L turn towards the Finstertaler Scharte, though waymarked, is
easily overlooked.

The perceptive will notice a small pass marked on AV map sug-
gesting an alternative to the usual transfer above; Längentaler
Scharte (2654m) lying between the Kl. Horlachsteinkar and the
Längental. It could be approached from R.10. Crossing N
over the pass (2h) and down to the small lake (2527m) is easy.
However, in mist and with no path, the final descent may be
difficult to find and the rock step must be turned R(E).

Hut connection: **Bielefelder**, R.10.

DRESDNER   2302m

DAV Sekt Dresden in Böblingen. Large modernised hut with
baths and showers situated at head of the Fernau valley.
With the advent of the Stubai Gletscherbahn, little used by
climbers; the residual clientele are walkers traversing hut to
hut. In summer therefore sometimes almost deserted at night.
Not surprisingly the alpine hut atmosphere has disappeared.
Historically this is a great pity as this was the first hut to be
built in the Stubai Alps, originally a "Schutzhaus" – literally a
shelter house.

In summer, below the snowline, the whole area between the
Lange Pfaffennieder to the E and pt.2992 on the Daunkogelferner to the W is a gigantic cirque of scree and boulders
with innumerable ski hoists littering the desolate landscape.
In places bulldozers have forged and flattened wide tracks,
leaving unsightly ribbons winding upwards. In 1987 a large
new complex came into use as an extension of skiing facilities at c2620m, W of pt.2624 at the site of an existing skilift
building. Access has certainly been speeded up for day trips
to nearby peaks by riding the Gondelbahn to the Eisgrat terminus (restaurant) at c2870m, though whether this constitutes
an improvement remains a matter of opinion. Sometimes path

markings are difficult to find because of new construction work but fortunately navigation is rarely a problem hereabouts. Not a pretty place in the summer.

b.1875, rebuilt 1887, enl. 1926, 1966, 1968. Tel: 05226-8112. Open: mid February – early November (except 10 days in June). B 70, M 130. Parking: Mutterbergalm. PT. Mutterbergalm (bus). Gletscherbahn middle station virtually outside hut door.

17　From roadhead at **Mutterbergalm** (restaurant, accommodation) a wide path leads SW, soon crossing over to W bank of the Fernau stream. It winds up grassy W slopes of the valley to hut (1h30-2h).

18　For the very popular traverse from the **Neue Regensburger** hut follow marked path SW up the valley towards the Falbesoner See. Just before lake the path divides (signpost). Take the L fork heading SSW over boulders and snow, finally S and steeply up over boulders to the Grawagrubennieder (2880m). If snow/ice covered this final slope, in good conditions waymarked and in zigzags, can be quite awkward and a rope may necessary (2h). Now cross broken rock slopes SW below the Gamsspitz SE face to the Schafspitz ridge at c2650m. The path continues W across a rock ridge to the Ruderhof cirque, then SW, passing below the Schafnock SE ridge before contouring WSW at c2500m. The Hölltalscharte track joins from the R here (see R.21). Later the comfortable path descends to cross the stream E of the Nördl. Daunkopf at c2280m before climbing again through an area called Wilde Grube to pt.2506, and finally descending ESE to hut (5-6h from Regensburger hut).

19　From **Sulzenau** hut take a marked path WSW to the W bank moraine of the Sulzenauferner. The track goes along it to c2580m, then winds steeply R(NW) up to the Peiljoch (2676m) in 1h30. Now descend a narrow cirque NW and a rock barrier N. Finally over scree slopes W and cross a small plateau, passing just S of the Gletscherbahn complex and up to the hut (2h in all).

A traverse of the Gr. Trögler provides a longer though more interesting alternative; a vague path branches NW soon after leaving the hut and leads steeply to the Kl. Trögler (2885m) then along broad ridge to the top and down W to join the Peiljoch route at c2410m, F- (3h30).
The views, particularly of the Sulzenauferner and Zuckerhütl, from either Peiljoch or Trögler, are superb.

Hut connections: **Amberger**, R.2. **Franz Senn**, R.21. **Hildesheimer**, R.27. **Hochstubai**, R.33.

FRANZ SENN　2147m

ÖAV Sekt Innsbruck. Large important hut on the Alpeiner Alp, serving as a base for almost all peaks in the Schrankogel- Ruderhofspitze-Lisenser Fernerkogel group. Named after the famous pioneering pastor. A more detailed note about the history of this well known base is given in Appendix A as its development is typical of many Alpine huts.

b.1885, enl. 1909, 1932, 1954, 1960. Tel: 05226-2218. Open: mid June - beginning October. B 84, M 160. Parking: Oberiss. PT. Oberiss (minibus service from Neustift). Cable hoist: Oberiss - dedicated telephone at lower station or ask at Oberiss Alm cafe.

20   The tarmac road from Milders in the Stubaital leads up the Oberbergtal to **Oberiss** (1745m). From here the path goes W, initially fairly flat over meadows, then climbs the steep hillside by zigzags to c2020m. (An alternative forks L before significant height is gained but it is more used in winter than in summer and indeed is referred to as the Winterweg; also very stony and often muddy). The hut soon comes into view in the distance, a pleasant photographic opportunity; the path leads along to R of the stream with little height gain, then a final short ascent over slabs before crossing stream to hut (1h).

21   From **Dresdner** hut reverse R.18 to the track junction at c2460m, NE of the Mutterberger See. Now go round the Hölltalspitze SE ridge and zigzag N up to scree cirque below the Hölltalferner which is not touched. The path is now little used and difficult to follow to the Hölltalscharte (3173m). **Serious stonefall has rendered crossing this pass difficult and dangerous.** The fixed ropes have gone. Originally aiming for one of the gullies reaching to the lowest pt. of the ridge, it is now difficult to locate the best gully from below or above, and in poor visibility there is no clue at all as to the best line upwards from the Hölltal. Presently (1989) the crossing is best avoided. On N side of the saddle the route descends 30m onto the Alpeinerferner and goes NW to join the normal ascent route for the Ruderhofspitze and so down R.148a.

22   From **Neue Regensburger** hut a path crosses slopes NE to foot of the Summerwäntl, then rises NNW over grass and scree slopes before winding steeply up to the Schrimmennieder (2706m). Now go down rocky slopes of the Platzengrube to the Kuhgschweg. Then round foot of the Uelasgratspitze and Östl. Knotenspitze N ridge, steering W to hut (3-3h30).

Hut connections: **Amberger**, R.3. **Potsdamer**, R.46. **Westfalen**, R.60, 58.

GROHMANN   2254m

CAI Sekt Sterzing. Also known as the Übeltalferner hut and Rif. Vedretta Piana. Tiny one-roomed stone building with corrugated roof situated on a rocky outcrops c100m above and N of a large basin draining the Übeltalferner. It operates as a satellite of the Teplitzer hut and is staffed from there. Occupied by the Ital. military for some years.

b.1887 (by Sekt Teplitz of DÖAV). Open: all July - end September (but was closed on occasion in August 1988; if necessary as part of an itinerary, check beforehand). No sleeping accommodation except in emergency; refreshments only. Parking: Roadhead above Maiern in Ridnauntal. PT. Maiern (bus from Sterzing). From **Maiern in Ridnauntal** by R.5.

Hut connections: **Becherhaus**, R.5. **Schneeberg**, see R.50/50a.

GUBENER-SCHWEINFURTER   2034m

DAV Sekt Schweinfurt-Guben. Referred to in text as Gubener hut though Guben is now partly in Poland and partly in East Germany. Situated at pt. where the Zwiselbach valley (Zwiesel) curves SW to continue downwards as the Horlachtal. A dirt road has been constructed from Niederthai though private cars are not allowed. A most pleasant and comfortable rather low-level hut surrounded by pasture.

b.1912, enl. 1963/64, 1974. Tel: 05255-5702. Open: mid June - end September. B16, M64. Parking: Niederthai. PT. Umhausen (bus). Also jeep/minibus to hut by prior arrangement with the tourist office in Umhausen.

23 A gravel road for vehicles runs all the way from **Niederthai** along N bank of the Horlach stream (unmarked on 1981 AV map). Much of the original path remains; after passing Larstigalm (1765m) it is more pleasant to stay on S bank of the stream till crossing quite close to hut (2h).

24 The signed route for the Gubener hut leaves **Winnebachsee** hut N along the lakeside, soon breaking L from the Westfalenhaus path (signpost). It rises generally NW through the Winnebachkar, red waymarks, snow patches higher up, finally over steeper snow and a narrow marked path on steep scree to the Zwiselbachjoch (2870m), 1h30-2h.
On the other side the descent curves gradually towards the NE on L of the Zwiselbachferner over boulders and snow patches, waymarked. In poor visibility and snow there is a useful large cairn at c2600m where the path turns sharply N. Thence an easy walk down to hut, crossing to R of the stream at c2250m. Just before the hut note 2 tracks R, the first at c2120m for the Gleirschjöchl and Neue Pforzheimer hut; the second at c2080m lies just before the cattle sheds and is the signposted, rather dull way to the Zwiselbacher Rosskogel (4-4h30).

25 From **Neue Pforzheimer** hut the marked path leads W then SW, finally steeply up to the Gleirschjöchl (2750m) - an easy crossing. Leaving this, zigzag steeply to descend into the Zwiselbachtal, turning NW at c2350m to join R.24 a few min. above hut (3h).

Hut connections: **Bielefelder**, R.11. **Dortmunder**, R.16.

HILDESHEIMER   2899m

DAV Sekt Hildesheim. Popular, friendly, old-fashioned hut
with a lot of atmosphere; situated in a fine position on rocks
W of the Pfaffenferner above a small lake - often frozen early
in the season. The quickest approach is from the Eisgrat
terminus of the Stubaier Gletscherbahn.

b.1896, enl. 1937, 1974. Tel: 05254-2300. Open: end June -
end September. B 25, M 50. Parking: Sölden. PT. Sölden
(bus). Cable hoist: from Schäferhutte - dedicated telephone
link to hut.

26   In **Sölden** cross river to the E bank, to the Sports Centre.
Turn R and follow this road, surfaced for a short distance, up
hairpin bends to a padlocked barrier at a hairpin; carparking
space. The motorable though unmade track continues through
woods high above the Windache stream to emerge on the pleasant
pastures just below Gasthaus Fiegl (1959m), accommodation (2h).
Note en route 4 paths signposted to the Hochstubai hut; 3 are
clearly marked on AV map, the second in order of meeting at
c1760m not being marked at all. After the Gasthaus, a short
descent and the track runs alongside the stream. A signed
route to the Brunnenkogelhaus crosses a bridge at c1940m. One
km ahead, just after crossing the Waren Bach where it joins
the Windache stream, a small little-used path rises steeply L (N).
This is unmarked but offers a route to the Windacher Ferner,
emerging on the glacier some 500m distant from and about 100m
below and SW of the Stubai Eisjoch.

The track now rises again to c2110m where the first of 2 possible paths to the hut breaks L from the Siegerland hut track
which continues generally E up the Windach valley. The first
option at c2110m is a little longer in distance, less steep and
more scenic, with zigzags large and small pushing up the hill
side. The second path goes L at the cablehoist station for the
hut (dedicated telephone) a few min. further up the valley.
This rises more steeply and more straight to join the first path
at c2720m. Just before hut, at c2820m, the connecting path
from the Siegerland hut arrives from the valley floor R; signpost (Sölden to hut, about 4h30).

27   (a) From **Dresdner** hut follow R.2 through an area called
the Gamsgarten until the track divides at c2630m a short distance E of the ski station complex. Rather faint red paint
flashes (presently) mark the stony track winding SSW to top
station of the Gletscherbahn-Eisgrat (2850m). Most people now
attain this pt. using the 'bahn. Next follow an obvious direct
line SSW to the col, walking alongside the skitow which goes
all the way to top. The track is marked by ropes to keep the
errant tourist away from crevasses L - there is more risk here
by straying R and being struck by downhill racers. The col,
usually called Eisjoch (3133m), is only a short way E of the

Bildstöckljoch which is no longer an easy crossing pt. A small
control hut for the skilift just below the col reduces further
the thus-far negligible mountaineering atmosphere. The way
onward is marked by posts and usually a beaten track SE over
the Gaisskarferner to rocks close to pt.3058; continue down
more rocks SE until a sharp turn SW round and above the
small lake. The hut is clearly visible for some distance beforehand, F- (about 1h from Eisjoch, 80-90 min. from Eisgratsta.).

(b)   The older but now rarely used route from the same hut is,
these days, more difficult to follow and takes the E bank of a
stream running SSW and marked as a path on the AV map.
Thereafter the faint path zigzags up scree and rocks (snow
patches) to reach the Fernauferner proper just below (NE) of
pt.2808 (incorrectly marked 2608 on AV map). Continue SSW
over the gently rising glacier, keeping the rocky outcrop R
and taking a direct line to the Fernaujoch (also known as the
Schaufelnieder) - small crevasses (3050m). Once over the col
go W then NW over broken rocks to the Gaisskarferner and
contour round at c3000m to join R.27a at the moraine bank.

28   From **Hochstubai** hut descend a few m to the Wütenkarferner
and head E then NE to the Warenkarscharte (3187m). Descend
(usually) broken rocks and snow onto the Warenkarferner. (In
July 1987 the first few m descent were quite difficult with some
ice, wind slab and even a modest cornice). Contour round this
glacier passing below, sequentially, Westl. and Östl. Daunkogel
before veering ENE along a corridor of snow between Stubaier
Wildspitze and pt.3004, gradually gaining height to arrive S of
the Stubaier Eisjoch at the col pt.3149. Then continue as R.27a,
F.   Route finding problems in poor visibility. Normally 3-3h30.

29   From **Siegerland** hut the signposted path winds generally
NW round the hillside, losing a little height, then going N and
NW into the cirque at foot of the Triebenkarlasferner. A small
glacier lake lies L as the path zigzags up towards the Gamsplatzl, a col at foot of the Geisskogel N ridge marked with large
cairns (3019m). The Hildesheimer hut is in sight NW from here.
Continue down again in zigzags across boulders below the Pfaffenferner (R) and down to the Gaiss stream crossed at c2750m.
(From the Hildesheimer this col looks dreadful for walkers, but
don't be put off - it's easy). After crossing the stream the hut,
150m above, is reached by a steep path joining the Sölden R.26
track at c2820m (signpost) (3h).

30   From **Sulzenau** hut follow R.19 but leave the track below
(SE of) the Peiljoch. Continue SSW to end of the moraine. Go
onto the glacier E of pt.2982 and climb steep slopes of its W
bank, keeping the Aperer Pfaffengrat close to your R-hand side.
Turn crevasses R. Above 3140m the slope eases off. Continue
in the same SSW line to the Pfaffenjoch (3212m) and reverse

R.109a to hut, PD-. There may be significant crevasse problems (4-4h30).

Hut connection: **Müller**, R.112, 111, 109 sequentially.

HOCHSTUBAI   3173m

DAV Sekt Dresden in Böblingen. Superbly situated atop the Wildkarspitze - the highest hut in the Austrian Stubai and the third highest in Austria after Erherzog Johann (Glockner) and Brandenburger (Ötztal). The Becherhaus on the Ital. side of the frontier is a few m higher. The hut has limited running water.

b.1931-1933 (opened 1938). No telephone, radio communication. Open: all July - mid September. B8, M38. Parking: Sölden. PT. Sölden (bus). No cablehoist, hut supplied by helicopter.

31   From **Sölden** leave the village as for R.26 past the carpark space on hairpin bend with the road barrier. About 350m up the road from there the Hochstubai hut path forks L and is clearly signposted. This is quite steep but well surfaced and pleasant through woods to Kleble Alm (Kleblar, 1985m); beds, food and superb views of the Ötztal glaciers. Note: before the Alm is a L turn for Stallwies; this joins the main Windach track at c1760m, see under R.26, unmarked on AV map.

After Kleble Alm the path goes E, less steeply and soon crosses open hillside to turn N into the Laubkar. Pass 2 path junctions, the first for Fiegl's Gasthaus at c2240m and soon afterwards, by a pool, the well signed path up to the Söldenkogel (easy walk, good path, fine views). Continue generally N, climbing on E side of the cirque to pass the small Laubkar See and to the Laubkar Scharte, old cablehoist (2760m). The path turns E here into the narrowing Durrenkarlen before climbing out NE over rocks and finally swinging round to approach hut from the N over snow, F- (5h).

There is an alternative, interesting though little frequented way from Fiegl's Gasthaus. Take the marked path NW, soon onto a smaller path NNE steeply in zigzags, passing E of the larger of the 2 Seekar lakes and up into the Oberer Seekar (emergency bivouac marked on map). This cirque is often snow filled. Continue generally N to gap at pt.3114, then W easily over snow to hut.

32   From **Amberger** hut leave S on the signposted path, level at first and on R bank of the river. After a few min. note the Kühscheibe and Aterkar Jöchl path leaving R (signposted "K"). At c2280m (40 min.) the path forks. Go R and ascend a rocky path quite steeply before a more gradual ascent to reach the glacier at c2700m. Then steadily up and S keeping close to flank of Wilde Leck and aiming for the emerging col

of the Wütenkarsattel (3115m) which lies immediately R of the
W ridge of the obvious and beautiful Windacher Daunkogel.
Some large crevasses just before reaching the col. The descent onto the Wütenkarferner is easy and the best line to the
hut is to curve L, slowly gaining height so as to approach
from the E aspect; finally ascend a steeper snow slope, F
(3h30).

33   Routes from **Dresdner** hut.
(a)   Traditional way over the Daunscharte. A messy route to
start with, now that skiing facilities have been extended. It
involves crossing a barren moonscape of boulders and mud to
get onto the Daunkogelferner. A better way is from the Eisgrat terminus of the Gletscherbahn either as R.33b or by going
up to the Eisjoch and joining the Hildesheimer-Hochstubai hut
connection described in R.28. However, if you are determined
or penniless then leave the Dresdner hut on a path W (signposted), crossing the stream where another track (for the
Regensburger hut and Hölltalscharte) forks R a few min. above
the hut. The path continues just S of W above the S bank of
the stream and leads into the desolate area at foot of the Daunkogelferner. Scramble over boulders, streams and sundry
other obstacles to join the glacier c2700m, then WSW directly
towards the Daunscharte (crevasses). A short steep snow
slope with a bergschrund to finish, usually best crossed well
to the L. On the far side a steep snow/ice slope with a bigger bergschrund leads onto the Sulztalferner. Head NNW down
to c2980m before turning SW towards the Wütenkarsattel - care,
crevasses of all shapes and sizes. Then follow R.32. F+,
about 4h30.

(b)   From the Eisgrat station walk W across snow to the rocky
outcrop pt.3013. Scramble up and continue generally W across
the upper Daunkogelferner - easiest above the crevasses and
keeping just below the rocky spurs of Östl. and Westl. Daunkogel - to the Daunscharte, F+. Shorter than R.33a.

(c)   Follow R.2 over the Daunjoch to the Sulztalferner. Move
across the glacier between c2960 and 3000m, keeping heavily
crevassed zone to your R to join R.32. From Daunjoch to the
Wütenkarsattel takes about 2h and a further 30 min. to the hut,
about 4h30 total, F.

Hut connection: **Hildesheimer**, R.28.

INNSBRUCKER   2369m

ÖAV Touristenklub Innsbruck. Most comfortable and, at the
time of writing, newly-rebuilt hut beside the Pinnisjoch at the
E foot of Habicht, and with a beautiful view of the Tribulaun
group. Excellent facilities including warm showers. Largely
used by parties doing the Habicht normal route, by those making

the interesting and by no means always straightforward transfer between Innsbrucker and Bremer huts, and Via Ferrata devotees pitting themselves against the new (1986) Ilmspitze Klettersteig.

b. 1884, enl. 1938, 1960/62, rebuilt 1982/83. Tel: 05276-295. Open: end June – end September. B 40, M 120. Parking: Gschnitz or Neder (bus). Jeep/minibus Neder-Pinnisalm. Cable hoist: Gschnitz, dedicated telephone at lower station.

34   From bridge over the Ruetzbach at **Neder** take road SE for a short distance to Schmieden at entrance to the Pinnistal. The track follows valley stream past Herzebenalm (1338m) to Pinnisalm (1559m) at 1h45. The latter can also be reached from top of the Elfer chairlift (from Neustift) in less than one h, and of course downhill. Thus far a pleasant enough valley with refreshments at all the Alms but with a dry streambed higher up. The path continues SSW to Karalm (1747m), drinks, where it steepens and finally zigzags to the Pinnisjoch. The hut is just over the pass on the R (SW), about 4h from Neder.

35   From **Gschnitz** walk SW up road for a few min. to where an obvious though small path leads WNW upwards along a small stream. It ascends, steeply at first, through scrub and meadows and later open slopes, gradually turning W under the Kalkwand, eventually crossing steep terrain by ledges to the Pinnisjoch and hut (3 h). An older path running more or less under the cable hoist from the Feuerstein Inn is steep and less often used.

Hut connection: **Bremer**, R.13.

MAGDEBURGER   2423m

CAI Sekt Sterzing. Also known as Schneespitz hut and Rif. Cremona alla Stua. Attractive and comfortable low wooden building sited on a rocky promontory E of the Stubenferner with fine views of the Rochollspitze, Agglsspitze and the Pflerschtal.

b. 1887, enl. 1898/99, 1904-06, 1970. Tel: 0472-62472. Open: end June – end September. B & M 50. Parking is limited – by river bridge in upper Pflerschtal at c1390m. For detail see under Tribulaun hut (Ital.). Extended road unmarked on ÖK 2710/2711. PT. Innerpflersch (also known as St Anton in Pflerschtal and St Antonio). Bus from Gossensass (Ital. Colle Isarco). Cable hoist: From pulley on L bank of stream just below Ochsenhutte. Ring hut beforehand from public tel. in valley and give ETA at pulley. They will look out for you with binoculars (honestly).

36   From carparking space in the upper **Pflerschtal** cross the stream and turn W, soon to arrive at path junction for Tribulaun hut at c1535m. Continue W on path No.6 above R bank of the Pflerschbach. Little height is gained till passing Ochsenhütte on your L. (Note: the unmade road from the carpark extends up L bank of the Pflerschbach, unmarked on ÖK 2710, and crosses

40

stream to R bank just below Ochsenhütte. The cable hoist pulley
is a few m beyond bridge on the L bank). Then climb more
steeply, generally NW, on a very stony path, eventually zigzagging up a small gorge to emerge at Schafalm pt.2116 (Schafhütte
on map). More zigzags follow; waterfalls L to distract attention.
The path keeps N, finally W, reaching the hut which appears at
the last moment (2h30).

Connections: **Bremer**, see note under Bremer hut detail.
Tribulaun (Ital.), R.57. **Teplitzer**, R.53.

MÜLLER   3143m

CAI Sekt Bozen. A hut with interesting origins. Originally
sited a little higher on the ridge behind the present structure
in 1891 by Sekt Teplitz DÖAV. At that time it was known as
the Erzherzog Karl Franz Joseph Schutzhaus. Subsequently
rebuilt on present site by the same section in 1907 and know
as the Müllerhütte after a certain Prof. Carl von Müller of Sekt
Teplitz. Why the title Pfaffenniederhütte was introduced is not
clear though the derivation is obvious. The hut fell into disrepair after the First War when the South Tirol became Italian
property and it was not until 1973 that it was reopened and
refurbished as Rif. Cima Libera.
Though fairly primitive and with no running water, the hut has
a pleasant homely atmosphere and is in spectacular glacier scenery on N edge of the large Übeltalferner, some 30m above the
glacier, on a small promontory at foot of the Wilder Freiger SW
ridge and just SE of the Pfaffennieder. Strongly recommended
for a visit.

b. 1907, refurbished/reopened 1973. Radio telephone. B 30,
M 40. Open: all July - end September.

37 From **Nürnberger** hut follow R.85 to summit of Wilder Freiger. Go a few m down rocks of the SW ridge, then descend a
snowslope S (often small bergschrund) before following the
glacier SW under the SW ridge down to hut, F (30 min.).

38 From **Sulzenau** hut, immediately on leaving cross the stream
E (signpost), as for traverse to the Nürnberger hut. Follow
red waymarks towards the Blaue Lacke where it joins the old
track destroyed by the 1987 floods. Then along the fast-dis-
appearing moraine ridge, aiming for lower part of the rock
shoulder reaching NW from Aperer Freiger. Get on to the
Fernerstube at c2700m, turning S at c2900m and, keeping clear
of crevasses L, continue towards the Wilder Pfaff E ridge. At
the last moment turn E to the Pfaffennieder, climbed by a short
scree/snow/ice slope. In summer 1988, a lean year for snow,
there was a moderate bergschrund and a fixed wire for assist-
ance up the ice slope. Much loose rock here, so look out for
parties above. Red flashes on the rocks can be seen on descent

from the col to the Fernerstube but these are not visible from below. A post on the Pfaffennieder itself is visible from a distance down the glacier; it bears the legend "Achtung Staatsgrenze". The hut is a few min. on the other side, bearing L on a waymarked track over boulders and snow patches, F+ (3 h).

Hut connections: **Becher**, R.6. **Hildesheimer**, R.112,111,109. **Siegerland**, R.116,114.

It is also possible to attain the Schneeberg hut by crossing the Übeltalferner to the Schwarzwand Scharte, descending SW to the Schwarzsee, then taking R.48. Alternatively one could use one of the routes from the Müller hut to Botzer (see Section 6) and continue by R.49. Neither are particularly interesting.

NEUE REGENSBURGER   2286m

DAV Sekt Regensburg. In the Falbeson valley with good facilities. The old Regensburg hut in the Dolomites was forfeited to the Italians after WW1. The upland basin between the hut and the Hochmoosferner was, like the Sulzenau Alm, threatened by hydro-electric developments (including a dam) for the Austrian State Railway. In 1988 this valley seemed likely to be reprieved.

b. 1930/31, enl. 1964, 1975/76. Tel: 05226-2520. Open: middle June - end September. B 26, M 70. Parking: Off the road just N of bridge at Falbeson, ample space. PT. Falbeson (bus). Cable hoist: Falbeson; dedicated telephone at lower station.

39 Leave the **Neustift-Mutterberg Alm road** at bridge over the Ruetzbach just N of Falbeson by the Waldcafe (restaurant). A marked path ascends wooded slopes NW in many short zigzags to a shoulder, Bei der Forche (1790m). Continue past the Falbeson Alm (Ochsenalpe, refreshments, 1818m), then W on the N bank of stream to a step which is surmounted well R of waterfall by zigzags to the hut (2h30). Note: Below Ochsenalpe the path on the AV map does not match reality. It crosses and recrosses the small road (no access for private vehicles) in an apparently random but well-signposted fashion.

Hut connections: **Dresdner**, R.18. **Franz Senn**, R.22.

NÜRNBERGER   2280m

DAV Sekt Nürnberg. Modernised hut with good facilities at head of the Langental. This small valley suffered severe damage in the 1987 floods. Besuch Alm was particularly badly affected. b. 1886, enl. 1898, 1908, 1962. Tel: 05226-2492. Open: middle June - end September. B 62, M 106. Parking: Small area on L of road about one km S of Ranalt at start of the approach route. PT. Stubaital bus stops at the carpark. Cable hoist: From Besuchalm; dedicated telephone at the lower station.

It definitely says "finish up the amusing wall."

40 About one km S of **Ranalt** on the Mutterbergalm road (c1375, small carpark, bus stop, signpost) the wide track goes S into the Langental. Go up valley on E side of stream; cross it just before reaching the Besuchalm (1572m); cable hoist station on opposite (E) bank of stream from restaurant. A few min. further S reach steeper ground. The path climbs SW in a series of zigzags, interrupted by a brief traverse SE, to c2000m. Continue S on the E slopes of the Mairspitze, finally steeper over rocky terrain, to the hut (2h30).

41 From **Sulzenau** hut take R.85b (for Wilder Freiger) to the N bank of Grünau lake. Now fork L and head NE. At c2500m near a cluster of small lakes the path divides again to give a choice of routes. Both ways involve some scrambling but the longer option (b) is easier.
(a) The R-hand fork leads E to a lake at c2530m and climbs steep rocks to the Niederl gap (2680m). The last bit is exposed, fixed cables. Now descend broken rocks and grass slopes E in short zigzags to hut, F- (2h30).
(b) The L-hand fork continues NE to pt.2742 on the broad Mairspitze S ridge. This top can be bagged without difficulty in 15 min. Then descend a rock rib E as far as pt.2553 and steep slopes SE to hut (3h).

Hut connections: **Becher**, R.8. **Bremer**, R.14. **Müller**, R.37.

PADASTERJOCH HAUS   2232m

Cosy, welcoming hut in attractive surroundings, situated on flattish ground near edge of a cirque SE of the Wasenwand. Also known as the Naturfreundhaus. b. 1907. Radio telephone only. Open: mid June - mid September. B 15, M 40. Parking: Trins (Gschnitztal). PT. Trins.

42 In **Trins** (Gschnitztal) park and/or start walking from the area of the village called Leiten; the hut is signposted from the village centre and at the carparking space. The track leads W into the Padaster valley on E side of the stream. At c1450m reach a major track junction; the waymarked path leaves the motorable track to cross an alp, recrossing the track at c1650m and thereafter frequently whilst zigzagging through woods. Easy to follow, it levels out near hut (2h30). A signposted option is to follow the track for all or part of the way.

43 (a) An interesting approach is from the **Maria Waldrast** inn, itself either reached on foot up the jeep road from Matrei (Wipptal) in 2h, or via the chairlift from Mieders (Stubaital) to Koperneck (1652m), followed by an easy 45 min. walk through woods. Start a few min. along the Matrei track S of Maria Waldrast, where the latter track turns E. Take the signposted Kalbenjoch path past Ochsenalm, up the valley SW to the Matreier Grube and finally steeply to the pass (2226m). The path now

contours SW and zigzags W up to a shoulder on the Kesselspitze
NE ridge which is followed to the top (2728m). The path continues SW, later S, along the broad ridge over the Roter Kopf
(2527m) to the N foot of the Wasenwand and rounds it L (E)
before descending SSE to the hut (5h).
(b)   From the Pinnistal follow the main valley track up to within
a few m of Issenangeralm. A tiny path (signposted "Naturfreundhaus") leaves L through woods to go behind (E) of the Alm.
It climbs very steeply over open hillside to the Hammerscharte.
This section of the route is called the Rohrauersteig. Descend
E from the Hammerscharte to intersect with R.82 between the
Schäferhütte and the Padasterjochhaus (4h).

NEUE PFORZHEIMER   2308m

DAV Sekt Pforzheim. Small hut on plateau at E side of the
Rosskar, and above and overlooking the Gleirsch valley. Also
known as the Adolf Witzenmann Haus. b. 1926, enl. 1967. Tel:
05236-276. Open: mid June – end September. B 22, M 50.
Parking: St Sigmund in Sellraintal. PT. St Sigmund (bus).
Cable hoist: From Ochsenhag immediately below hut beside the
river; dedicated telephone.

44   From the bus stop in **Sankt Sigmund** (Sellraintal) take the
surfaced track S into the Gleirsch valley. Soon the way becomes
unsurfaced but remains motorable all the way up to Ochsenhag
(2132m) where the Materialseilbahn for the hut is sited. Between St Sigmund and there, notwithstanding passing a watering
hole at Gleirschhöfe (1662m), a generally uninteresting walk.
After Ochsenhag cross the stream W and climb steeply in zags
to the hut, in sight all the time now, eventually approaching it
from the N (2h). Note an alternative approach from Praxmar in
the Lisenser valley over the Satteljoch on a marked path.

Hut connection: **Gubener**, R.25.   **Westfalen**, R.170.

POTSDAMER   2012m

DAV Sekt Potsdam-Dinkelsbühl. An attractive hut in the Fot-
chertal above the Seealm. b. 1931/32, enl. 1966/68. Tel: 05238-
2060. Open: mid June – early October. B 18, M 32. Parking:
Alpengasthof Fotsch (1520m). PT. Sellrain (bus).

45   The road from **Sellrain** is open for motor vehicles for 6 km
as far as the small Fotsch hotel. Note however that it may **not**
be used at certain times on Sunday afternoons and public holidays. From the Fotsch hotel take the wide jeep track on L of
the stream through woods. At c1650m a small path branches R
signposted "Sommerweg" and steadily gains height up largely
open hillside with occasional trees. This is a much more attractive route up this pretty valley than following the track used by

jeeps servicing the hut. The latter is situated on a small plateau above the Seealm a few min. after the Sommerweg and track merge (75-90 min.).

46   From **Franz Senn** hut take marked path NE. This divides twice, first at c2200m where the Rinnensee path goes L by a waterfall, then 500m further on at c2220m where the Horntalerjoch path forks L. The R-hand path continues NE across the Schafgrübler E spur and into a cirque, the Viller Grube. (Here where the path is running N and just before the first significant stream, an old path with faint red flashes runs down directly and safely to Oberiss). The far side of the Viller Grube has a short stretch of somewhat exposed path "protected" by fixed ropes of doubtful safety in 1987. The path then contours as far as Seedug Alm where again it divides (R fork to Seejöchl). Go L (NW) steeply up to the Wildkopfscharte (cairn, signpost, 2585m). On the other side of the col go down steeply, well marked, to cross the Fotscher stream close to pt.2015, then contour along the NW side of valley to the hut, passing a crossroads en route (L for Hochgrafljoch and Lisens, R to Seealm below the hut). About 4h for the transfer.

Note: A signpost at the Potsdamer hut indicates a time of 5-6h for the walk to the Franz Senn. This is both depressing and misleading. 4h or a little more should be ample.

SCHNEEBERG   2355m

CAI Sekt Meran. Also known as Rif. Monteneve. It lies in the W corner of a basin immediately S of the aptly named Schneeberger Weissen. An extraordinary and fascinating place, rather reminiscent of an Alpine Blaenau Ffestiniog. Mining took place at Schneeberg from as early as the 13th century, particularly for zinc, silver and lead. In 1962, after mining had ceased, the miner's canteen was taken over by the CAI as a mountain hut. The frontage has surely been used as a set for filming Ital. (spaghetti) Westerns. All the other buildings of what had been a thriving community are now in disrepair. The hut staff are very welcoming and the food excellent but the best that could be said about the accommodation in 1987 was that it was extremely indifferent and the author, given the option, would bivouac.

Taken over, 1962. Open: all June - mid October. B 15, M 39.

Parking: Roadside at Schönnaralm in the Passeiertal. PT. Moos in Passeiertal (bus).

47   From **Timmelsjoch Pass** road at Schönnaralm take the marked track (Path No.31) heading NE and later N, climbing steeply to reach a small lake with some disued mine buildings at the foot of an incline. Here the track turns sharp L before resuming a N then E course to the hut, reached up broad mine tracks and adorned with a large crucifix in a little under 2h.

48   From **Siegerland** hut a path is marked on AV map to the
Windachscharte.   Though initially waymarked and cairned as it
goes SE across moraine of the Östl. Scheiblehnferner, it disap-
pears some distance from the base of the steep gully leading to
the col in a tangle of loose boulders.   Late in the season with
no snow in the gully there is considerable stonefall.   Pick the
best line and make sure no-one is above you.   On far side of
the col descend quite steep scree and snow, ultimately an obvious zigzag path, down to the pretty Schwarzsee (Timmelersee)
where it intersects with the Timmelersee to Schwarzwandscharte
route.   Round the lake S and take up the marked path, shown
petering out on AV map, in an area called "In der Mute". Traces
of path and occasional red/white flashes here; some amusement
to be had searching for them as they are cunningly concealed.
Where the AV map path ends go S to pt.2477, keep R of pt.2462
and pass E end of a small pool.   Then trend SW before turning
S to the Gurtelscharte.   Always keep screes below the glacier
of Schneeberger Weissen to your L and aim somewhat L of the
obvious Gurtelspitze (Gurtel = belt, and clear even from cursory
glance at mountain).   Nearer the col the way is plainer and better marked.   Maps give different opinions as to the position of
the Gurtelscharte, either L or R of the actual crossing at the
lowest pt.   Nonetheless the path to our col is obvious and crosses at c2680m; this concurs nicely with a pass marked on the
AV map.   Now go SSE steeply down over boulders and round
the S aspect of Schneeberger Weissen when the hut will come
into view below (3-3h30).

49   From **Becherhaus** follow R.125b, moving L to cross the Bot-
zerscharte, then contour S across the glacier (latter is unnamed
on AV and ÖK maps but on other maps is confusingly called the
Rötenferner; the AV map cites a Rötenferner immediately S of
the peak).   Now move down SE across a small rockband, then
scree to foot of the AV map's Rötenferner before turning SW
and down again to c2700m.   Follow messy boulders/snow to the
Nördl. Schwarzseescharte (2857m); a pole marks the col.   Now
down an obvious though little used steep path to the Schwarzsee.   At c2600m SE of the lake the path divides (L fork to the
Schneebergscharte).   Take R branch which quickly becomes
hard to follow.   Beware of a steep waterfall and move generally
SW down the valley keeping the stream to your L.   In good
visibility the hut is seen from the lake; in bad conditions you
will come across ruined buildings by the stream just below the
hut, F (3h).

50   From the roadhead above **Maiern** in the Ridnauntal, pass
through the disused mine buildings and go L (SW) along the
signposted, marked track under the 2 now defunct cableways
originally used to transport miners and materials between the
valley and the mines above Moareralm.   It is an old miner's
road and passes through pleasant countryside, crossing the
Lazacherbach to its N bank almost immediately and reverting

to the S bank at c1570m. This road is shown in its entirety
on ÖK 2710. At c1950m, just after the disused cableway top
station, it is easy to miss the divergence of the route L then
up to the disused Kasten Wirtshaus (also shown as the Posch-
haus or Post-hütte) with the nearby smallholding across the
stream at Poschalm (2h). This "junction" is not signposted nor
clearly defined on the ground. A little upstream of Kasten go
W across the stream and an obvious path leads up a broad valley to the Kaindljoch (c2675m) where there are some old buildings. Note (a) that this pass lies just N of the Schneebergsch.
which accommodates a smaller path, and (b) ÖK 2710 shows some
cableways which have now been dismantled. The hut lies about
1.5 km down the other side with about 350m of descent along the
a clear track (5-5h30). At c2500m you may see the remains of
the "Kaindlstollen", the tunnel under the Schneebergscharte used
by miners and, until recently, the public. It is now impassable.

50A   An interesting walk is worthy of inclusion, good in its own
right though could be used as an unusual approach to Botzer and
Hochgwänd or as a connection between Schneeberg and Grohmann/
Teplitzer huts. After passing Kasten-Wirtshaus (R.50) follow red
waymarks and a signpost for the Egetjoch (2681m) which lies between the Schwarzseespitze and Moarerspitze. It is not accurately
shown on ÖK 2710 but rises gradually N from behind the Poschalm
before turning W into a shallow green valley graced by a pleasant
limestone stream. Subsequently the path is accurately marked on
the AV map, turning N and climbing W of the pretty Moarer Egeten
See to the pass (4h so far). The N side is less steep and winds
easily down to the E of the attractive Trübersee, still clearly waymarked, to drop more steeply and cross the stream just below
2180m. In 1988 there was no bridge; just a rushing stream and
cold wet feet. The next river crossing over a gorge immediately
below the Grohmann hut is more conventional though the bridge
itself is less so (6h from Maiern).
If traversing from or to the Schneeberg hut one can cut off the
corner between Kaindljoch and Egetjoch, leaving R.50 on a small
path at c2450m and contouring round the hillside to join R.50A
roughly where it turns sharply N below the Moarer Egeten See.

SIEGERLAND   2710m

DAV Sekt Siegerland. Somewhat unusually shaped hut with
turret-like corners situated at the SW foot of the Sonklarspitze
amongst the desolate remains of the Östl. Scheiblehnferner.
b. 1930, enl. 1971-73.   Tel: 05254-2142.   Open: all July - end
September.   B 26, M 50.   Parking: Sölden. PT. Sölden (bus).
Cable hoist: From c2392m, dedicated telephone at lower station.

51   From **Sölden** follow R.26 to the lower station of the Hildesheimer hut Materialseilbahn. Here the wide track becomes a path
clearly waymarked along N bank of the Windach stream. The hut
soon comes into sight, far too soon you might feel. The path

later crosses the river at c2340m and subsequently meanders through a boulder maze, the exact route probably changing annually. It passes the Materialseilbahn station for the hut (pt. 2392, telephone), then goes steeply up the final 320m. A long tedious walk with the bit around the Gasthaus Fiegl the only really attractive part (4h30-5h).

Hut connections: **Hildesheimer**, R.29. **Müller**, R.114 and 116. **Schneeberg**, R.48.

SULZENAU   2191m

DAV Sekt Leipzig in München. Interesting site atop a precipice above the Sulzenau Alm. One of the most pleasant of all hut approaches, quite short and through varied terrain. A few min. up the Peiljoch track, small climbing wall on some rocks with colour coded routes and secure pegs. b. 1926, enl. 1939,1958. Destroyed 1975, rebuilt 1976-79. Tel: 05226-2432. Open: all June - end September. B 30, M 120. Parking: Grawa Alm. PT. Grawa Alm (bus). Cable hoist: From Grawa Alm; dedicated telephone at lower station; minimum of 5 rucksacks carried.

52   Just beyond Grawa Alm (spectacular waterfall) by pt.1590 (bus stop, roadside parking), the track crosses L over river off the **Mutterberg Alm road.** Zigzag through woods, generally SE, up to W bank of the Sulzenau stream. Continue SW through a narrow defile, crossing the stream twice, to the Sulzenalm at 1847m. The restaurant here is interesting because of the amusing carved chairs and fence posts. In 1988 this attractive flat basin was under threat of hydro electric development to service the Austrian State railways. A little further on the path, still SW, climbs steep slopes by a series of zigzags to avoid the cliff below the hut. At c2100m the path trends S and soon winds up SE to the hut (1h30-2h).

Hut connections: **Becher**, R.8 and R.85b. **Dresdner** R.19. **Hildesheimer**, R.30. **Müller**, R.38. **Nürnberger**, R.41.

TEPLITZER   2586m

CAI Sekt Sterzing. Also known as the Feuerstein hut and now, correctly, as Rif. Vedretta Pendente. Barn-like, wooden slatted building on a rocky plateau just S of the Hangender Ferner with nice views W over the Übeltalferner and good hospitality. Down the cliff immediately S of the hut is the Grohmann hut, easily reached by a good path (R.5, 20 min., read appropriate note to see lack of facilities here). Badly damaged by lightning in 1986 but now fully restored. For many years was closed to tourists because of occupation by Ital. customs officials.

b. 1889. Tel: 0472-66256. Open: all July - end September. B 35, M 50. Parking: Roadhead above Maiern in Ridnauntal. PT. Maiern in Ridnauntal (bus from Sterzing).

53   Leave **Magdeburger** hut on the marked path that leads W towards the S branch of the Stubenferner. This glacier has regressed enormously and is no longer accurately portrayed on maps. Particularly later in the season there is little snow below 2800m. For this reason the recommended route to the Südl. Stubenscharte has been redirected and in places now strongly resembles the Miner's track from Pen y Pass to Snowdon. Some will consider this a work of art, other will merely note the diligence. Having left the way indicated on map at c2600m, the path stays on rocks S of the glacier to emerge immediately W of pt.2817. It is only a short distance from this arrival on snow to the col (2931m), 1h30, where you turn SW into a rocky basin on N side of the Feuersteinferner. The path narrows, following ledges with fixed ropes and some exposure, turning NW just N of pt.2854. Eventually there is a dramatic and steep downward exit onto the glacier L, awkward despite a cable. (In the reverse direction this departure from the glacier may be difficult to find in poor visibility. The clues, apart from judicious use of the compass, are a height of c2880m and a site some 100m R of a narrow snow gully which falls from the Schneespitz SE ridge. Similarly, for those wishing to cross into the Gschnitztal, the couloir up to the Pflerscher Niederjoch may be difficult to locate). Cross the glacier WSW, almost level to begin with, then increasingly steeply to the snow covered Magdeburger Scharte (3105m), with S ridge of the Westl. Feuerstein to R and N ridge of the Agglsspitze to L. The quickest way down to the Teplitzer hut is not as suggested by the AV map. Keep L of the obvious rock island (stonefall to R) and at c2840m turn sharply S, keeping pt. 2834 to your R, and move round E side of the small lake shown on map to pt.2830m. Here pick up a well marked path (not on map), leading to hut. First, it goes S over rocks, then turns gradually NW, keeping pt.2676 to its L, to emerge just E of another slightly larger lake (on map, alongside the S projecting tongue of the Hangender Ferner) whence it resumes a southerly course to hut, F+ (5h).
Note: Going in the other direction it is still feasible to push N from the hut, just W of the lake, then straight up to the glacier before turning E.

For access from the **Ridnauntal** at Maiern, see R.5. See also R.5 for connections with **Becherhaus** and **Grohmann** hut.

For a direct connection with the **Nürnberger** hut, the Enges and Weites Türl offer quite easy access from the Hangender Ferner from the S, but the exit N onto the Grüblferner can be extremely difficult, particularly for the Weites Türl. An easier alternative lies further W at the Rotgratscharte.

TRIBULAUNHAUS (Austrian)   2064m

TVN Sekt Innsbruck. A new hut sited on a promontory at N foot of the Gschnitzer Tribulaun, a few m away from site of the

original hut destroyed by avalanche in winter of 1974/75.
b. 1978. Tel: 05276-252. Open: mid June - end September.
B 2, M 40. Parking: Feuerstein (Gschnitztal). PT. Feuerstein
(bus).

54   At **Feuerstein** a signposted track leaves the valley road SE
immediately on the Gschnitz side of the bridge over the Sandesbach. Some carparking space along riverbank on this short
track and ample a little further up the main valley road.
A path now zigzags steeply L of the waterfall, the gradient easing as the Sandes valley opens up. Steep zigzags recur about
1840m to take the path to a small plateau on which the hut
stands (2h).
An alternative though less pleasant way is to use the motorable
track which starts by the carpark at the end of the road in
Feuerstein. This keep W of the Sandesbach until W of and below
the hut, where it turns through 180° to approach from the S.
Very boring, hard on the feet and probably no quicker in either
direction.

55   From the **Ital. Tribulaun** hut follow marked path NW, then
up to the Sandesjöchl, also called the Pflerscher Scharte on
some maps including ÖK 2710 (2603m), 30 min. A well marked
path descends steeply NNE before curving E then N to hut
across boulder slopes below Goldkappl and Pflerscher Tribulaun
(1h30).

Note: It is important not to confuse the Sandesjöchl with the
Sandesjoch, a small col lying between Pflerscher Tribulaun and
Goldkappl. Also that a new path was constructed in 1987 between a pt. just N of and below the Sandesjöchl and the Bremer
hut. It was sponsored by the DAV Sekt Bremen and called the
Jubiläumssteig. It takes 5-6h and was not marked on available
maps in 1988.

55A   An alternative connection uses the **Schneetalscharte**. Quit
the Ital. Tribulaun hut SE to a path junction after 10 min. Reverse R.56b (using pathNo.7) until the next path junction c2060m
is reached (30 min.). Instead of descending SE along path No.7,
continue along the Pflerscher Höhenweg (path No.32A) which
winds somewhat precariously round limestone cliffs, fixed ropes
in places and plentiful Edelweiss - a protected plant.
When the path finally climbs into the Koggraben valley it intersects with the Innerpflersch-Schneetalscharte path (No.32); it
is straightforward to turn N and ascend towards the Schneetalscharte (No.32 goes on to the Portjoch). Quicker still, turn N
at a slightly earlier unsigned path junction c2060m; this avoids
crossing the stream, thereby saving height. It slants diagonally up rocks (fixed ropes) and eventually meets path No.32 at
c2300m. In descent on this side of the pass this junction is·
clearly indicated on nearby rocks - "Pflersch" to L, "Tribulaun
H" to R. Finally quite steep scree goes up to the Schneetalscharte (2645m), 3h.

Note: If you intend to include Gschnitzer Tribulaun or the Schwarzwandspite in the outing, consult the appropriate route details before attaining this pass - it may save irritation. If simply crossing the pass then follow instructions for the Schwarzwandspite - accurately shown on ÖK 2711.

The Austrian side of the Schneetalscharte is a nasty place unless (a) covered with snow or (b) you enjoy scree. Avoid using this side in ascent unless in snow. The red waymark painter has sprayed the word "Scheise" on a rock near the top. The meaning is not known but is believed to agree with the general sentiment. It is otherwise an easy and fast descent to the Tribulaun Haus in 45 min, F-.

TRIBULAUN (Ital.)   2368m

CAI Sekt Sterzing. More correctly Rif. Calciati al Tribulaun. In an interesting position beside the Sandes lake, dominated by the S/SW walls of Goldkappl and Pflerscher Tribulaun. A small and unpretentious hut, Ital.-Colonial in appearance. b. 1892, rebuilt 1960. Tel: 0472-62470. Open: all July-end September. B 19, M 29. Parking: A new road (unmarked on ÖK 2710 available 1987) runs S of the Pflersch stream from Innerpflersch (St Antonio) up to a bridge at c1390m; some carparking space. From here the surface is unmade but cars are permitted to a tiny and unofficial space, room for 8-10 cars, by bridge at c1465m. This river crossing is marked on OK 2710, W of and above Stein. The view of the Pflerscher Tribulaun S wall from here is superb. PT. St Antonio, bus from Gossensass (Ital. Colle Isarco).

56 (a) From **Innerpflersch** (St Antonio) follow new road on S side of river and in just under 3 km reach carpark noted above. Cross river on marked path which then turns W, dividing at c1535m - Magdeburger to L, Tribulaun to R (No.8). The path now crosses open meadows before zigzagging steeply through scrub and crossing a stream beside a small waterfall just above 1800m. Cross a rocky shoulder (shrine and seat) at c2000m; the immense face of Pflerscher Tribulaun comes into view. Continue NE to junction with R.56b (No.7) just before passing 2300m. Then easily NW to reach hut in 10 min. (2h30).

(b) An alternative way starts behind Innerpflersch church by path No.7, sharing the initial ascent into the Koggraben with routes to the Schneetalscharte and the impressive local waterfall. At c1525m branch L from the Schneetalscharte path and soon cross the river before continuing generally NW, mounting all the time, to join R.55A (part of the Pflerscher Höhenweg) at c2060m immediately below the Pflerscher Tribulaun face. Continue round base of mountain, still ascending, to join R.56a just below 2300m just after crossing a boulder/scree slope (stonefall danger from above). This route is relatively little used and, though well waymarked, is grassy and overgrown in places.

I wouldn't use the wire - it's not fastened at this end.

57   From **Magdeburger** hut descend slightly NE to cross the
Stubensee outflow stream, then almost immediately fork L (not
further E as AV map suggests) and follow waymarked path
No.7 over boulders round the Schafkampspitze S ridge and
turning N into an appallingly stony cirque. With frequent
spring stonefall the way may be difficult to follow here but
generally aim at the SW corner of the Weisswandspitze, arriving on a broad ledge/terrace that runs across the southern
aspect of the mountain, identified by the change in colour of
the rock and by snow patches. This section can be tricky if
there is much residual snow. In dry conditions it is a safe
though mildly exposed path suitable for walkers. The sheer
drop a few m R (S) would mean special care with children in
the party. After rounding the Weisswandspitze reach a col
with a rocky knoll pt.2860 before ascending the Hohe Zahn or
High Tooth (2924m), passing only a few m S of its highest pt.
Now down the E ridge to a cairn at c2800m, turning L (NE)
here down slabby rocks to join the ridge again at c2750m;
good views L into the Gschnitztal; all along here you face
Goldkappl and Pflerscher Tribulaun. Finally down boulders
and snow patches into the bowl of the Sandes See, joining the
descent path from the Sandesjöchl (see R.55), no signpost, at
c2450m. In sight the hut lies a few min. below (3h30).

Note: The round trip of R.36, 57 and 56a is a reasonable day
excursion of say 8h with rewarding views. Either direction is
suitable, that above offering rock enthusiasts a limestone won-
der to gaze at, though the opposite way may be preferred to
avoid going up the stony cirque which is much less tedious in
descent.

Hut connection: **Tribulaunhaus** (Austrian), R.55.

WESTFALENHAUS   2273m

DAV Sekt Münster. Situated on W side of the Längental below
the Grubenwände, about 150m above the valley floor. Comfortable
and well equipped, with showers. b. 1908, enl. 1930,1970. Open:
mid June – end September. B 15, M 44. Parking: Lisens. PT.
Gries im Sellraintal (bus). Cable hoist: From Fernerboden on
winter ascent route. Dedicated tel. at lower station.

58   From **Lisens** (1636m), sometimes Lüsens locally, large parking area, Gasthof but no shops, in the pretty Lisensertal, the
wide summer track leads up W side of valley. Just before crossing stream at c1720m the main track turns back N to Praxmar and
is not marked on current map. The signposted hut path branches
L and ascends steeply through woods passing a higher junction
with the upper level path from Praxmar at c1920m. Soon the path
turns W over open hillside easily to hut (2h). Note that the winter track follows the valley floor S to Fernerboden (1716m), the
lower station for the cable hoist, then turns W upwards through

trees following the Fernaubach. After passing the Längental Alm and crossing the stream the path rises steeply to hut.

59 From **Winnebachsee** hut follow the marked and signposted path N along the lakeside taking the R (signposted) fork c2380m where the Zwiselbachjoch path leaves L. Follow attractive stream up into the less attractive and boulder strewn Winnebachkar; turn E and later NE over boulders and snow of the Winnebachferner to the Winnebachjoch (2788m), 1h30. On far side of the col descend a steep but short snow slope, thereafter following well marked way E through the desolate Ochsenkar to hut (1h, 2h30 total).

60 From **Franz Senn** hut take R.145 to the Horntaler Joch. Descend the steep Gr. Horntal on the R side, later turning N away from it at c2300m and coming down NW through woods into Lisens. Thereafter follow R.58.

Note: It is also possible to traverse from the Westfalenhaus to the Franz Senn or vice-versa by getting onto the Lisenser Ferner, using the Brunnenkogel Rinnen of which there are three, numbered 1 to 3 from N to S. The southernmost is the easiest, emerging by the rocky island in the Brunnenkogelnieder which lies between the Hint. and Vord. Brunnenkogel. This col is not named on AV map though all the Brunnenkogel Rinnen are. Note that none are recommended crossing pts. because of loose rock and stonefall. Another possibility is to go up to the Längentaler Joch (R.4), thence traverse the Hint. Brunnenkogel (R.140, 139, 141).
Hut connections: **Amberger**, R.4. **Pforzheimer**, R.170.

WINNEBACHSEE   2362m

DAV Sekt Hof. Pretty little hut situated on Winnebachsee itself in a fine position at E foot of the Gänsekragen (qv). Beautiful waterfall view from the terrace. Much of the accommodation is original. b. 1901, enl. 1960,1983,1986. Tel: 05253-5197. Open: all July - end September. B 8, M 20. Parking: Gries im Sulztal. PT. Minibus Längenfeld - Gries (inquire Reiseburo Maurer, Längenfeld). Cable hoist: from Winnebachhof. Dedicated tel. from bottom station.

61 From carpark at E end of **Gries-im-Sulztal** take the track NE along the Winnebach stream up to Winnebach hamlet. The actual way and number of fences to cross varies from time to time depending on the whim of the landowner (or take the longer way on the obvious metalled road). The signposted wide track goes out of the hamlet onto a forestry road winding quite steeply up through woods to continue as a smaller path in more open ground above and NW of the Winnebach stream. Eventually zigzag over rockbands, a beautiful waterfall distracting attention from the gradient, until the hut appears suddenly round a corner L (2h).

62   From **Amberger** hut go N down the Sulztal, crossing river at
the Hint. Sulztal Alp huts.   Shortly, a signpost indicates the way
towards both Winnebachsee and Westfalen huts, up into the Schrankar, very steeply at first and gradually turning E and NE into
the wide basin of boulders and sometimes snow patches.   Pass 2
small lakes, pt.2688; ahead lies a signpost at c2720m where the
red waymarked path to the Gaisslehnscharte breaks L (straight-
ahead lies the Längentaljoch for the Westfalenhaus, R.4). From
here the track is not marked on the AV map (1984).   It goes
just N of W, immediately S of the small lake pt.2755, over a
bouldery knoll and up over snow patches and more boulders to
the Gaisslehnscharte (3054m).   A snow/scree gully leads down
to the Bachfallenferner.   Travelling in the reverse direction the
entrance to this gully is clearly spotted with red and yellow
paint.   Descending the glacier, keep broadly R, curving down
to get onto rocks just S of the small glacier lake below 2680m.
A short climb over boulders leads to a signpost for the Grüne
Tatzen route to Hoher Seeblaskogel R, and to the Winnebachsee
hut L.   Coming in the opposite direction the legend "Amberger
Hütte" is painted on rocks indicating the direction.   From here,
about 40 min. down to the hut.   Overall rather tedious in ascent
through the Schrankar and better in the opposite direction.   A
useful hut connection nonetheless, F (4-4h30).

Hut connections: **Gubener**, R.24.   **Westfalen**, R.59

Section 1 TRIBULAUN GROUP

AND OTHER PEAKS EAST OF THE SCHNEESPITZ

This group constitutes the E end of the Hauptkamm. Rock climbs here are among the best in the region, of all grades and on limestone. From the Schwarzewandspitze 2 ridges extend NE and SE on either side of the Obernbergtal. The latter branch is of no interest to the climber. On the NE ridge there is a little excitement once N of the Eisenspitze, though the NW wall of the Mutte or Muttenkopf (2637m) offers a climb of IV in about 2h30 from Gschnitz into the Rossgrube.

OBERNBERGER TRIBULAUN   2780m

Scree pile E of the Schwarzewandspitze. Can be reached on a path over its E slopes from the Obernberger See in 3h. A short section is quite loose, mildly exposed and protected by a "fixed" rope that was very much unfixed in 1985. In spite of this it is a genuine walk. There is a straightforward connection to the Schwarzewandspitze in 1h. A N face route is graded IV.

SCHWARZEWANDSPITZE   2917m

Rock peak E of the Schneetalscharte with an impressive NE face and a good view of the main Tribulaun group.

West Ridge. The most frequented way and a good scramble, F.

63   (a)   From the Austrian Tribulaun hut take marked path SE into the Schneetal; the Gstreinjoch track soon breaks L. The way then turns S between the Eisenspitze L and Gschnitzer Tribulaun R, rising finally quite steeply on scree/snow to the Schneetalscharte (2643m), 1h30. The col is divided into 2 by a rocky hump. Take the L-hand one; this choice is clearly marked on ÖK 2711. The few hundred m below the col is a gruelling and miserable ascent in the absence of snow.
      (b)   From Innerpflersch go up the village road to the church. A few m beyond, a signposted path goes R, ascending R of the waterfall. At c1525m a path forks L for the Ital. Tribulaun hut. After this the way zigzags steeply NNE into a rather forbidding valley with steep rocky cliffs close R. Above c2200m the direction changes to NW in a rocky basin to finish fairly steeply at the scharte (3h). See also detail under R.55A.

Now climb W ridge with some fixed cables towards a secondary top which is turned L (N). A 10m vertical step is tamed by cable and iron spikes. The ridge steepens near the summit (1h30 from scharte).

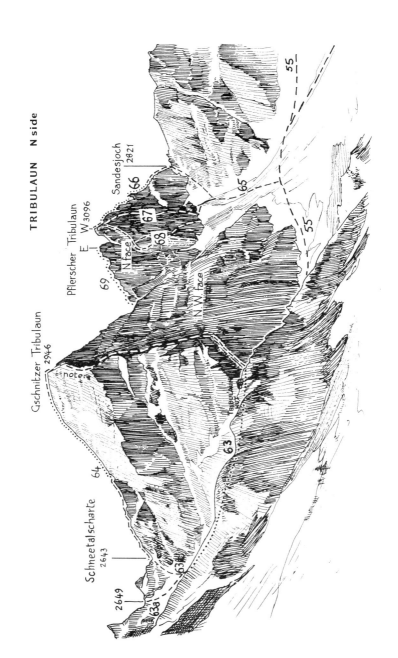

TRIBULAUN N side

Schneetalscharte 2643

Gschnitzer Tribulaun 2946

Pflerscher Tribulaun W 3096

Sandesjoch 2821

noten

E

N face

N.W. face

2649

631

63ll

64

63

65

55

55

66

67

68

69

EISENSPITZE   2673m

Sharp rocky peak S of the Gstreinjoch with a variety of rock
routes.   The E face is II though usually used in descent.   The
rock is notably loose.   All can be conveniently approached from
the Austrian Tribulaun hut.

GSCHNITZER TRIBULAUN   2946m

Overshadowed in fame, ease of recognition and height by its ill-
ustrious neighbour; nevertheless an impressive NW face. The SW
ridge from the Tribulaunjoch (that between Gschnitzer and Pfler.
Tribulaun) is II though the col is difficult of access from Austrian
side.   Of several routes possible on the NW face, none is currently considered worthwhile.   FA.   G.Pittracher, 1872.

East Ridge.   Straightforward from either side of the frontier
and a rewarding top if the ascent of the Schneetalscharte from
the N doesn't deter, F.

64   From either the Austrian Tribulaun hut/Gschnitztal or Innerpflersch use R.63 to reach the Schneetalscharte.   From the N
side use the part of the col R (W) of the central rocky hump.
Approaching from the S there is a red direction arrow some 30m
or so below the pass, taking you L (W) round a rocky spur and
up a loose gully to the col W section.   From the scharte scramble
up following obvious marks towards a small chimney with an un-
necessary and sometimes unattached fixed rope.   Afterwards, a
gentle rising walk over limestone to the top, following a cairned
path along the broad ridge (45 min.).

PFLERSCHER TRIBULAUN   3096m

Jewel of the area, a magnificent and unusually shaped mountain with 2 main peaks (E and W).   The traverse between the
2 is IV and takes 2h.   All routes to the less frequently visited
E peak are quite difficult and many plagued by stonefall; the
best way is by the NE ridge from the Tribulaunjoch (IV+, 2h),
the col between Pflerscher and Gschnitzer Tribulaun.

South Face.   The ordinary route which uses upper part of the
face.   Fixed ropes on the steepest pitches make it easier.   Some
loose rock with consequent stonefall danger, PD/PD+.   FA.
N.Winhart, G.Hofmann, G.Pittracher, J.Grill, 1874.

65   From the Austrian Tribulaun hut take the track SW as for
R.55 over scree towards the Sandesjöchl.   Leave this at c2150m
to head S up scree and occasional snow patches steeply to the
Sandesjoch (2821m), between Goldkappl and Pflerscher Tribulaun
(2h30).   The Sandesjoch can also be reached from the Ital. Tribulaun hut in 1h30 by going into the hollow below and climbing a

steep gully. (Note, the Sandesjoch and Sandesjöchl are very
different places. The latter is also sometimes known as the
Pflerscher Scharte). Next go to SE round foot of the NW ridge
to a steep rock ledge about 7m wide; traverse E along it as far
as a small outcrop. Then follow a narrower scree ledge E to its
end by a drop and climb a couloir to reach another ledge. Go
through a narrow gap R to a short scree slope. Near the upper
E side of this slope reach a 5m overhang. Climb it by a wide
chimney which narrows near the top (fixed rope) and continue
up a steep slabby gully. Bear slightly R to a corner surrounded by almost vertical rock N and W below the final wall. Go
up this for 60m (III), initially very steep with fixed ropes, to
the NW ridge then turn R to reach summit quickly (5h from
Austrian side, one h or so shorter from the Ital. start).

North-West Ridge. Also called W ridge, better rock than R.65,
not much longer and therefore used more frequently. AD. FA.
O.Melzer, E.Spötl, 1901.

66 To the Sandesjoch as for R.65. Now E up ridge to a
chimney-split tower leaning L. Climb chimney (III), slanting
L at the top, to a notch. Then abseil 20m from a block into
gap after tower. Keep R (S) of crest on ledges and gullies to
reach a double-headed tower. This can be turned R (S), longer, or climbed by a steep narrow chimney on its N side (III)
to a small col/gap. Again take to S side on wide ledges to yet
another gap. Go up 3m, move onto the N side to a steep broken
crack and via this (III+) reach crest again. Then straightforward to the top (5-5h30 from Austrian side,1h less from Ital.)

North-West Face. The well known Rainer-Eberharter route lies
here. Quite loose and not without danger; some pegs in place,
TD, crux pitch VI+. FA. July, 1945. Solo: Andi Orgler,1982.
Robert Troier, who made the 5th ascent in September 1985, provided the detail.

67 From the Austrian Tribulaun hut follow R.55 towards the
Sandesjöchl; leave this path over scree slopes to reach foot of
face (see R.65). R of the main peak fall line lies a usually snow
filled gully with an outcrop on its L below the main wall. Either
climb steeply L of outcrop or go up the gully and traverse back
L until below 2 parallel vertical cracks. Climb the R-hand one
to a wide ledge below the buttress roofs (cairn). Either climb
an overhanging crack on R side of buttress to a prominent rock
flake; or traverse 20m L on L side of buttress and climb a short
pitch to a good stance - from here go R along a rising ramp to
the rock flake. Now straddle across onto the overhanging face.
Slant upwards to a stance at a gashed boulder. Now, 80m above
the flake but further R, climb a dark crack to arrive below a
roof. Traverse 3m L to a chimney and climb it. Above, move
into a steep groove; overhangs block the exit; climb their L
edge strenuously until the angle eases. Continue fairly steeply
to summit (7h from hut).

E ridge 70

2809

< abseil point

< Sandesjöchl

Rebitsch-Frenademetz

GOLDKAPPL S FACE

Nordpfeiler Route. Though not on absolutely solid rock, still considered by some the best climb on the N face. Mostly V, some VI, one pitch VI+. FA. A.Orgler, F.Larcher, 1982.

68   Approach as for R.67. Start L of R.67 where, on the somewhat indistinct buttress, a series of fissures lies just L of a water channel. Above, to R of the striking curved edge, the wall is interlaced by cracks. The route follows these more or less straight up towards the W summit. About 5h from foot of face.

North-East Ridge to E summit. Climbed from the Tribulaunscharte, the col between Gschnitzer and Pflerscher Tribulaun, easy of access only from the Ital. side. AD/AD+. FA. E.Spötl and O.Melzer, 1901.

69   From the Tribulaunscharte go along ridge to the first tower which is turned on NW side. Go back up to ridge, occasionally moving down R, until you reach a striking yellow-coloured tower. This and the subsequent teeth are turned on R. After a further short distance on the ridge go L before next tower into a steep gully and back up to ridge again. Another deviation off the ridge NW follows, this time along a tricky sloping gangway, approaching the final steep bit. Climb down 20m L via a gully, then past an overhang R to yet another gully which is taken and by its L wall attain the E summit (IV), 2h.

GOLDKAPPL   2809m   (2793m, 2781m)

Smallish but finely shaped sharp rock peak with no easy ways. It lies just E of the Sandesjöchl (Pflerscher Scharte); there is cartographical disagreement as to its height. At least 7 well-described climbs involve handling some very dodgy rock. Indeed because of this the routes are done infrequently: the W ridge from the Sandesjöchl is III (2h30), staying largely on the crest with an occasional diversion onto the N flank. This is easier in ascent than in descent when the best way may be difficult to find.

East Ridge. Described here largely to permit a traverse and as a descent route for climbs on the 2 major towers of the E ridge, themselves usually climbed from the S. This ridge is also about III and loose.

70   From the Sandesjoch climb directly over the first 2 towers. The 3rd (Mühlsteigerturm) is circumvented on its S side via an exposed gully. After a gap the 4th (Flöckingerturm) is rounded N. Next over an easy stretch of ridge, a short pitch of III, then a flat bit to a small col. A short deviation on the S side attains a wide gully; go up this to small pinnacle that is the E forepeak. Keep on the S side subsequently to main peak (1h30 from joch).

South Face. 2 of the most famous and notorious rock climbs in the Stubai lie here. The Rebitsch-Frenademetz (1936) has been described by some as rewarding and by others as desperate because of loose rock. Nevertheless it is becoming increasingly popular after many years of being regarded as too difficult and dangerous. It includes 3 pitches at VI; poor protection in the lower half, especially near the crux 10 pitches or so up. The route, as described by Robert Troier, is shown in the photograph. The Veitstanz route (FA. H.P.Eisendle, H.Kammerlander, 1982) starts at the same pt. as the Rebitsch but goes further L and finishes on the W ridge. It has 3 pitches of VI and one of VI+.

Descent from both is initially down the E ridge for about 150m to a gap where there is an abseil pt. Then S into a system of gullies veering L to foot of the wall.

The Ital. Tribulaun hut is only a few m away from the start of the climbs and in the hut are good explanatory diagrams and photographs of the more recent and difficult routes, including those above.

Both Mühlsteigerturm and Flöckingerturm have well known S face routes, "Bänderriss" and "Tatzelwurm" respectively. FAs by Hans Peter Eisendle in 1979 and 1980 they are at V/V+ and the rock is fair. Good descriptions of these are also available in the hut though they are infrequently climbed.

PFLERSCHER PINGGL   2766m

Minor rocky top quite popular with scramblers. A vague path leads up E ridge from the Sandesjöchl, F (1-1h30 from col). See R.55. **Hoher Zahn.** Insignificant ridge top between the Pflerscher Pinggl and Weisswandspitze. The Tribulaun-Magdeburger connecting path (R.57) passes close to the summit – a mere stroll away.

WEISSWANDSPITZE   3018m

Limestone pyramid with a gneiss base. The N slopes fall steeply into the Gschnitztal. The easiest way up is by R.57 from either the Magdeburger or Tribulaun huts until due S of the summit, then up a broad slope, F (2h from Magdeburger, 3h30 from the Tribulaun). An alternative from the Austrian side is either (a) from Laponesalm by grass and steep scree sopes to Hoher Zahn (2925m), then descend W to saddle between it and the Weisswandspitze; or (b) by R.57 reached from the Austrian Tribulaun hut and Sandesjöchl. Both attain this saddle; then take E ridge, rounding pinnacles first S and later N (II); not recommended (1h30 from saddle).

SCHAFKAMPSPITZE   3016m

Rarely visited, more a long ridge, E of the Nördl. Stubenscharte (or Bremer Scharte). No straightforward routes. The N ridge is III (3h30 from Bremer hut), but the approach through Hohen

Boden is very tiresome. The W ridge from Nördl. Stubenscharte is mostly II with one pitch III, 2h30 from col; the latter is most easily reached from Magdeburger hut (see R.94). This ridge is almost 3km long and involves traversing lots of humps and small gaps. the E ridge is II from the Magdeburger hut using R.57 towards the Tribulaun hut as far as the Schneesumpf and, tiresome, to the col pt.2839. Finally over 3 rock teeth to the top.

Sod the book Jeff!

Section 2 HABICHT - SERLES GROUP

Extends NE from the Simmingjöchl to Habicht, and bounded by
the Stubaital to the NW and the Gschnitztal to the SE. After
Habicht the ridge divides, enclosing the Pinnistal; the lesser
portion leads roughly N and terminates at the Elferspitze. The
large, more important branch continues NE before itself veering
N to finish abruptly with the obvious Serles. The geological
structure differs on either side of the Pinnisjoch. Whereas the
ridge from the Wetterspitzen through Habicht to the Elfer group
consists of gneiss rock, the NE continuation from the Pinnisjoch to Serles is composed of Dolomite limestone. This is an area
well known for some excellent walking, some hard rock climbs,
the best known ice climb in the Stubai, and an emerging reputation for Klettersteige (Via Ferrata).

INNERE WETTERSPITZE 3055m

Most southerly top in the group, offering a small selection of
easy climbs and scrambles. The best are from the Bremer hut
and Simmingjöchl - described below. The N ridge descent way
is not recommended in ascent because of the tedious approach
from the Lauterer See. FA. P.Gleinser, W. von Lauterer, 1875.

71 East Ridge. PD-. From Bremer hut take the Simmingjöchl
path for about 200m before turning W at a signpost. With some
old red flashes on the rocks, the way leads gently over grass
amongst boulders and between small pools. Soon the ground
rises more steeply to a shoulder and the path continues still
over grass but now with occasional scree to a confrontation with
a conspicuous deep gully at c2750m. Turn R (N) and in a few
m emerge on the E ridge at a stance atop the deep couloir (1h).
Now established along the right line for the summit go up L
through a fissure above the gully to exposure rendered safe
with fixed ropes (in descent this might be difficult to locate).
Gentle grassy slopes follow to another small col where the ridge
is taken again. Follow crest or turn it more or less at will L,
traces of path, some loose stuff on the flanks, never more than
II, to the nice top (about 2h30 from hut).

In descent take the N ridge and keep just off the crest L. Do
not go down as far as the Lautererseejoch; this is difficult to
down-climb. Leave the ridge at c2950m via one of 2 couloirs,
just before it drops sharply to the col. Emerge on a boulder
field below and, lower, go down L side of the Schneekachel -
a small snowfield - quite a brisk glissade in good conditions.
A tedious boulder maze finally leads to the Lauterer See. Here
pick up the old Innsbrucker-Bremer hut connecting path, now

little used and not marked on AV map which quickly goes to the hut - complicated only by a steep ascent of some slabs - fixed ropes make this easier (2h down, 4h30-5h for round trip).

The S ridge from the Simmingjöchl (1h from Bremer hut, 2h from Nürnberger hut) is of similar standard. Cross a depression pt.2741 and turn the subsequent pinnacles R (E). Continue to turn steeper sections R. Slabby rocks lead to lower summit. Keep L (W) of crest to a knoll, then almost level to top (1h30).

ÄUSSERE WETTERSPITZE   3070m

Encompass within a traverse of both Wetterspitzen or climb singly from the Bremer hut. FA. G.Pittracher, N. von Kaun, 1881.

72   Reverse R.71 to the Lauterer See. Contour NE, traces of old path and cairns, ultimately aiming for small col pt.2590m on the E ridge. Cross ridge and go WNW and WSW up boulderslopes and slabs to the N ridge, then 10 min. along this to top (3h from hut).

Wetterspitzen Traverse. From the Simmingjöchl via S ridge of the Innere Wetterspitze and descent to the Lautererseejoch. Then up the Äussere Wetterspitze by its SW ridge (II); turn first steep step L (W) - direct = III, then stay on ridge over pt.2833 and 2899 to summit (2h from Inn. Wetterspitze). It is easiest to complete the traverse by reversing R.102. Altogether, 6-7h.

Südliche Rötenspitze (2982m), **Nördliche Rötenspitze** (2926m),

Ochsenkogel (Ochsgrubenspitze) (3033m), **Zwerchwand** (2912m),

Glücksgrat (2954m), **Grosse Glätterspitze** (3134m)

Peaks on ridge between the Äuss. Wetterspitze and Habicht; they are rarely climbed and have little to offer except solitude. All can be reached without difficulty from the Innsbrucker-Bremer hut path. Rock generally poor, difficulties occasionally III but mostly I or II. Traversing the lot was first done in the 1920s.

HABICHT   3277m

Handsome mountain which looks much larger than it really is because of its separation from other large Stubai peaks. Once considered the highest pt. in the Tirol and one of the earliest tourist climbs in the area, preceded only by, of all things, Strahlkogel in 1833, also by Peter Carl Thurwieser. FA. P.C. Thurwieser, I.Krösbacher, 1836 by the now normal E side route.

East Side Ordinary Route. A marked path with fixed ropes in places, some mild scrambling, very popular, F.

NW side HABICHT

3277

75

3176

3010

Mischbachferner

74

75

Alm

73   A signposted path starts just outside the Innsbrucker hut,
between it and the Pinnisjoch.   It ascends W and SW before turning up quite steeply NW over slabs; fixed ropes here.   Further
up a sharp change in direction SW (see below) takes the marked
route up a rocky ridge alongside the small Habichtferner before
the usually tracked and short transverse crossing of the glacier
NNW to the final ridge to the summit; more fixed ropes (2h30).

There is a dreadful history of fatal accidents, almost one a year
recently, on descent of this normal route - the result of trying
to cut the corner when crossing the glacier SSE in descent, ie
going too far L (E/NE) and aiming directly for the point of
change of direction indicated above.   Here the glacier narrows,
becomes much steeper and sometimes icy, and terminates in a
precipitous snow filled gully falling to the Pinnistal.   The safe
way when going down is to stick to reversing the accepted way
up and to use a compass in mist.

Mischbachferner Route.   Generally considered the most important ice climb in the Stubai Alps, very popular among the locals
and strongly recommended.   AD+ direct, up to 60° possible, but
with easier alternatives.   FA.   W.Pfurtscheller, O.Biermann and
F.Löwl, 1883.

74   Mischbachalm (1850m, sleep in hayloft) is reached on a marked path from the main Stubaital road between Krössbach and
Gasteig.   Start up a jeep track from the main road where there
is ample parking space.   The path zigzags alongside the Grab-
lasbach and turns S, up through woods before descending to the
Mischbach.   After crossing the stream the path goes up a wooded spur SE before turning S over meadows just before the small
hut.   From the Alm go up through the Äussere Mischbachgrube
and across scree and rocks.
Initially climb rocks R of the snow before crossing to middle of
the glacier (crevasses).   Now aim for the crux, the ice bulge of
the glacier's E arm, an icefall of c.80m, best taken on the L
along the edge (R side of bulge is slightly easier).   This leads
to a glacier basin below the summit ridge.   More crevasses here,
best avoided L before bearing S/SW up snow/ice W of the summit (bergschrund), some rocks near the top, to arrive on ridge
joining R.75 quite near the cross (5-8h from Mischbachalm,
depending on conditions).   An easier variant takes a rock rib
R that divides the glacier, thus avoiding the icefall.   Even
easier is the snow slope R of the rib.

75   Mischbachgrat (Westernmost N ridge).   Not as hard as the
Easternmost N ridge.   AD-.   FA.   H.Delgado, K.Hargspiel,1921.
From Mischbachalm (R.74) head SE up grass and rock strewn
slopes of the Äussere Mischbachgrube towards a pt. just below
the glacier snout.   Climb loose rocks W to crest and go directly
towards the first knoll.   Continue along ridge, traverse 2 teeth
on slabs (III, exposed), moving L onto the flank, returning to
crest at a gap before climbing the next tower directly (III). The

next flight of slabs can be turned L well down the Mischbachferner side with various ways for rejoining the crest. Now a narrow horizontal section before a sharp gap and another tower climbed by a groove (II). Descend to a saddle then steeply up ridge again without difficulty to a corner W of the peak; now more easily along broad ridge to top (6h from Mischbachalm).

Easternmost N ridge. Long and quite difficult, AD/D, climbed infrequently, starting from the Mischbachnieder (2642m) which is reached from Mischbachalm.

76 South-West Buttress. Rises to pt.3200 S of Habicht and gives a good technical climb. FA. I.& W.Reder, H.Weber,1951. From Innsbrucker hut take R.13 (Bremer hut path) as far as the Glättergrube. Head NNW up into the cirque to foot of the buttress at c2850m below the Glätterferner. Round a detached tower R. Behind it a loose gully leads almost up to a slight depression on the buttress. Keep below the crest. A few straightforward pitches on sound rock with plenty of holds precede an overhang (IV-). Climb it up to the crest which is followed over some minor pinnacles. Below the next step traverse 2m R into a strenuous 15m groove (IV+, crux). Move R out of it and climb steep smooth slabs (III+) for 35m until the difficulties ease and it is possible to slant L back to crest. Go up it to pt.3200 (3h30-4h). From here, either cross the upper edge of the Habichtferner NNE to join the normal route, or go over the glacier NNW to the summit riser. Climb a loose gully R of the ridge, round an overhang R on a ledge and climb steep slabs (III-, 20m). Return to crest and follow it to top (1h for this, say 5h from hut).

Manteler(spitze) 2824m   Sharp rock peak on ridge N of Habicht. S ridge from the Mischbachnieder is IV. Other routes are tedious and the flank approaches prone to stonefall.

Kaldererspitze 2690m   Little frequented peak on the ridge N of the Manteler. Easy ways up but uninteresting.

Zwölferspitze 2562m   The penultimate peak on the ridge. Easily climbed from the Zwölfernieder either by the NE ridge or roughly from the E using a small col between the main peak and N shoulder.

ELFERSPITZE   2499m

Last peak in the chain lying between the Pinnistal and Stubaital, N of Habicht. Nicely seen from Neustift. A straightforward and interesting walk from the privately owned Elfer hut which is 20 min. above the top station of the Elferlift - a 2-seater chairlift from Neustift - on a path (1h30). Paths also lead round base of the mountain on both Pinnistal and Stubaital side to the Zwölfernieder whence another track leads back down into the Stubaital via Autenalm (café). Indeed the whole area is interlaced with paths.

The name Elferspitze is reserved specifically for the highest pt. Elferkogel is used as an alternative title. N of our peak lie the Elfertürme (towers) with their precipitous W and N walls; Nördl. Elferturm (c2495m) and Südl. Elfertürme (c2490m). The latter S towers lie W of the Elferscharte and are designated W and E. When adopting the normal approach to the Elferspitze from the N you first pass the Nördl. Elferturm on your R(W) side just before the Elferscharte. There are a large number of short rock climbs mostly on the S Tower. These are up to VII- in difficulty (details in the AV Stubai Alps guide). One classic Elfer climb is described here.

Western South Tower – North Wall Route. A steep and fairly difficult climb on good rock with pegs in place. FA. Span, Stern, 1985.

77   Follow the Nordwand Klettersteig path (see below) until you get to the western S tower. The climb starts 5m R from pt. where you reach the tower. Follow obvious crack for 30m to a good stance (V). Go up 15m R over a slab below an overhang (V+) to another good stance on a ledge. Follow ledge L under an overhang, subsequently using a higher ledge continuation for 15m. Now straight up through a shallow scoop to platform (15m, III+). Climb trending slightly R, under a roof (crux,VI) passed R using a crack to a ledge with a stance (35m). Turn the next overhang L then go up between 2 roofs, closer to the R-hand one, and up a crack to top (IV+, 30m). Rpt. Luis Töchterle.

Elfer Klettersteige.

Klettersteige (Via Ferrata) are simply a series of metal rungs and spikes firmly fixed to the rock to allow total security while climbing, using both rungs and rock to stand upon. The equipment required for the venture includes a helmet, harness and 2 rope or tape slings each with 2 karabiners – so that the climber should be tied onto one of the rungs with one of the slings at all times.
There are 2 Klettersteige on the Elfer. The Elferkogel climb traverses the Elferspitze from the Elferscharte to Zwölfernieder, the col between the Elferspitze and the Zwölferspitze. This is recommended as an introduction to the activity (1-2h).

The W component of the S tower has the Nordwand Klettersteig. This is dramatic and exposed, somewhat prone to stonefall and recommended for the more experienced. The start is reached via a signposted path forking R from the main Elfer hut to Elferspitze path, keeping N of the Elfer massif until arriving under the N wall. At this pt. an alternative path continues SW towards the Zwölfernieder.

Kalkwand 2564m   Highest pt. of a jagged ridge ENE of the Pinnisjoch. A small signposted path leads from Innsbrucker hut across the NW flank, up to the SW ridge and approaches summit cross from the S (1h). The SW ridge itself is a good scramble on sound rock direct from the Pinnisjoch, II (1h). There are a number of rock routes on the W wall; the Central West Wall climb is recommended and on good rock, pitch of VI. FA. A & M. Orgler, 1981.

ILMSPITZEN

3 peaks NE of the Pinnisjoch, divided by deep clefts in steep walls which fall into the Pinnistal. The peaks are of similar height and have a high reputation for difficulty on sound rock. Only the newer NW and W wall climbs attract much attention and that largely from local climbers. More recently the excellent and very exposed Klettersteig has attracted enormous custom. The climbs are approached either from the Innsbrucker hut or directly up scree from just above Pinnisalm, very steep and tedious.

Innerste Ilmspitze c2690m

The southernmost peak. There are at least 6 recommended routes at grades between V and VII.
United Artists. FA. A. & M.Orgler, 1982. Considered the best climb on the Ilmspitzen. 300m, one pitch VII, the rest mostly above V, 5h.

78 Just R of the Ilmturm, and therefore R of R.80, the climb starts another 5m R of obvious fissures in the flake above and at a parallel crack. Go up this for 15m (V+), then traverse L into the main crack (VI). Continue by this to its top at a ledge (100m, IV/V+). Now traverse over the flake chimney and get onto the main wall 30m R and to R of 2 obvious water streaks. Climb 15m slanting L using small cracks (VI), then 10m R (VII), another 5m slanting L upwards to a chimney and climb it to some small towers. Next go L up a shallow corner (V+), at the end keeping L to ascend smooth slabs (VII-). After 10m sloping up R under a small roof (VI-), go R of roof to climb small cracks to a ledge. Now another corner with a crack, then an overhang to gain the next ledge. From here easily using N ridge to the top. Descent is by using the same ridge down to the flake, then abseiling into the Ilmturm cleft.
The SW ridge of this peak is more or less identical to the Klettersteig described below.

79 Ilmspitze Klettersteig. A good equipped route, hugely exposed, 300m high and not for beginners. Follow Kalkwand path along the NW aspect of the Kalkwand ridge, soon crossing to SE side via a small col. Below summit of the Kalkwand go R and down slightly along a new path which keeps just below the NE running ridge to a small equipment hut. The start of the route is somewhat concealed in a cleft on the southern aspect of the mountain. From the hut to the top takes about 3h. In descent follow the ascent route down until a sign indicates the round trip variation.

ILMSPITZEN

Äuss. 2692 Inn. Inn'ste

Ilmturm

N ridge descent

80 78
81

Kirchtürl

NW side
PINNISTAL

Ilmturm c2550m

A yellowish tower under NW wall of the Innerste Ilmspitze, just
R of the chasm separating Innere from Innerste peaks. It is
separated from the mountain by a cleft and can be climbed via
the cleft at about IV.

80 West Wall (Fankhauser Route). FA. H.Fankhauser,
A.Schlick, 1968. Start a few m R of deep cleft separating the
Ilmturm from the Innere Ilmspitze. From foot of the wall a
prominent and somewhat overhanging fissure leads under the
first roof. Now make a short traverse to L border of the roof,
then about 2m upwards to a stance by a chockstone. The ensuing small overhang is taken direct (crux, VI-). Now follow the
crack upwards for 40m to another stance (pegs). Subsequently
interesting climbing to the obvious shoulder. From a wide ledge
there go R over rock steps to a large boulder on the edge. Behind this go through a gap in the W wall to another stance, then
follow the wall more easily (IV) to top.

Innere Ilmspitze   2692m

81   Just a Walking in the Rain. Considered the best rock climb
on this peak. One pitch VI-, otherwise IV and V. FA. A.Org-
ler, 1982. L of cleft behind the Ilmturm is a bulging lower section of the wall about 80m high. R of this is a fissure which is
climbed to its top. Next take the R edge of an 80m high pillar
to its top, then go R for 15m on a ledge to a series of cracks.
Ascend these and the following chimneys, about 120m to ridge,
which is taken to summit.

The N ridge (III) is about 800m long and straightforward though
the first 50m is taken immediately L of the crest. Then stay on
ridge entirely, apart from turning 2 towers on their N side in the
upper part. A good descent route.

Äussere Ilmspitze 2690m   Northernmost of the 3 Ilmspitzen, seldom climbed and no recommended routes.

Torsäule   2645m

Really the SW shoulder of the Kirchdachspitze with a fine S face
that falls into the Gschnitztal. The normal route from the SW is
II but difficult to follow. The rock is thoroughly unreliable, the
face 600m high and the approach from Gschnitz long.

The Kirchtürl is the first obvious col on the ridge extending NE
from the Aussere Ilmspitze towards the Kirchdachspitze. The
subsequent small peak is the Kirchtürlspitze. Rock teeth on the
ridge between here and the Kirchdachspitze are known as the Kir-
chtürme. None have worthwhile climbs.

KIRCHDACHSPITZE   2840m

Obvious peak between Habicht and Serles with a particularly impressive NW face above the Pinnistal, frequently ascended by the
easy ways, especially R.82.

82   North-East Ridge.   The ordinary route, marked path and a
simple scramble, F-.   The track leaves the Padasterjochhaus S,
gaining little height then turning W past the Schäferhütte and
underneath the Hammerspitze before turning SW up to pt.2428
and going up the ridge to top (2h).   Alternatively leave hut by
same path and after a few min. turn W up to the Hammerscharte,
traverse the Hammerspitze (2634m), also called Riepenspitze,
without difficulty southwards and down to join the normal route
at pt.2428; a little longer than the first option.

83   Normal route from Pinnistal.   From Pinnisalm follow the main
Pinnistal track for about 500m to a signpost "Jubiläumssteig".
Cross the usually dry riverbed and follow the well marked path,
new in 1977, with fixed ropes in places.   It climbs 2 walls and
generally follows an obvious slanting line to emerge at a small col
just N of summit (3h from Pinnisalm).   No rock climbing but exposed in places; some might prefer the security of a rope; thus,F.

If starting from Neustift-Neder a round trip in a day is a long
walk with considerable height gain.   For those determined enough,
consider returning from the summit using the Hammerscharte (see
R.43b).

The NW and N face routes are demanding and currently unfash-
ionable.   The most recommended climb is the W Buttress route,
one pitch V+ but mostly IV, V.   FA.   A. & M. Orgler, 1981.

Wasenwand 2563m   Grassy slopes to the S with a rocky N face.
About 45 min. from the Padasterjochhaus - a short diversion from
the track leading towards the Kesselspitze.

Roter Kopf 2527m   Grass covered hill on track from the Padasterjochhaus to the Kesselspitze.

Kesselspitze 2728m   Rock peak with an impressive N face falling into the Pinnistal.   On the path N from the Padasterjochhaus
(2h), or from the NE from the Maria Waldrast Inn via Ochsenalm
and the Kalberjoch (2226m).

Lämpermahdspitze 2595m   Just N of small col between the mountain and the Kesselspitze, often called the Mauernjoch.   From the
Mauernjoch the SW ridge is II in 30 min.   S from the Rote Wand
it is straightforward.

Rote Wand 2524m   Small rocky hump immediately SW of the
Serlesjöchl, reached in about 30 min.

The whole area N and NE of the Padasterjochhaus, especially

around Blaser (2241m, path to the green summit) and the Peilspitze (2393m, also a path to top), is ablaze with flowers in the
spring and early summer. Walks in this area are excellent for
training, for photography or just for fun. The walk from the
Padasterjochhaus N along the above summits is a particularly
pleasant and straightforward outing.

SERLES (WALDRASTSPITZE) 2718m

Dominating junction of the Stubaital and Wipptal above Schönberg,
this is the easily recognised final peak of the Serleskamm which
reaches N from the Pinnisjoch. Apart from the normal route given
below, seldom climbed because of atrocious rock.

South-West Ordinary Route. A pleasant walk from Maria Waldrast
inn with a scramble to finish above the Serlesjöchl. More tiresome
from Kampl or Medraz in the W up scree slopes to the same col.

84 (a) The Maria Waldrast inn and monastery to the NE of Serles
can be reached on foot by a jeep road from Matrei (2h). Rather
easier is by way of the chairlift from Mieders in the Stubaital to
Kopperneck (1625m), followed by a gentle 45 min. walk through
the woods. From the inn the marked path rises SW through the
woods then scrub, gradually turning W and finally NW up to the
Serlesjöchl.
(b) From Kampl a track leaves the main road on the N bank
of the Höhlebach to rise steeply through woods to the restaurant
at Wildeben (1781m) where it joins the jeep track coming up from
Medraz. After Wildeben the way is well marked, ESE and later
steeply up scree slopes to the Serlesjöchl (2h from Maria Waldrast,
3h30 from Kampl).
From the Serlesjöchl the path is rougher with fixed ropes in places
but straightforward over scree and rocks to top (1h from col).

Section 3 EASTERN HAUPTKAMM

WILDER FREIGER TO SCHNEESPITZ AND ASSOCIATED PEAKS

WILDER FREIGER   3418m

A beautiful mountain shaped like a roof-top and set amidst the
largest glaciers in the Stubai. The lower SE summit is called
the Signalgipfel (3392m) where there is a ruined customs hut.
The ascent is extremely popular and the summit panorama vast
– one of the best in the Stubai.   FA. (by ordinary route)   –
F. Leis and companions, 1865.

North-East Ordinary Route. By far the most frequented way.
Approaches from the Nürnberger and Sulzenau huts converge
at the Seescharte, a saddle at foot of the Urfallspitze SSW
ridge. F.

85   (a) From the Nürnberger hut, more commonly used for
this route than the Sulzenau, head S on a marked path over
large rocks. The Simmingjöchl route branches L after a few
min. (signpost). Soon the path climbs in steep zigzags, up
underneath the Urfallspitze E flank towards the Seescharte at
2762m (1h30).
      (b) From the Sulzenau hut the path goes generally E,
soon losing some height to cross the Sulzau stream before rising SE to the Grünausee (2330m) (1h). After rounding the
lake N continue SE over rocks and snow patches to the Kleiner
Grünauferner, thence to the Seescharte to join (a) just on the
other side of the col (2h).

From the Seescharte continue SW below the Urfallspitze-Gams-
spitzl ridge on the easy to follow path. S of the Gamsspitzl
cross the N edge of a snowfield to reach the Signalgipfel NNE
ridge, NNE of pt.3065. Follow rocks, sometimes snow, over
this and pt.3127 to pt.3222 where the rocks end. Go S up the
glacier (small crevasses in late season), passing L of pt.3324
before heading SW over pt.3313 to the Signalgipfel.   The easy
snow ridge with a few rocks on your L leads quickly to the top
(3h30 from Nürnberger hut, 4h from the Sulzenau).

Though some parties do not rope up – indeed people have been
seen in training shoes – conventional glacier tactics should be
used; crevasses exist, particularly at c3240m though they are
usually snow-covered in July and early August.

South-West Flank.   The trade route from the Pfaffennieder,F.

86   From the Pfaffennieder cross boulders and sometimes snow
patches along a path in a few min. to the Müller hut. Follow
glacier immediately below rocks of the SW ridge until just SW

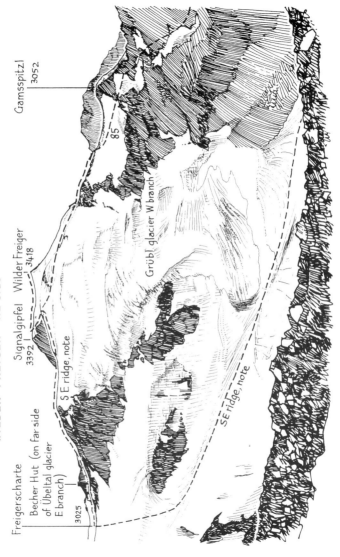

WILDER FREIGER   NE side

Gamsspitzl
3052

85

Signalgipfel   Wilder Freiger
3392   3418

Grübl glacier W branch

S E ridge, note

SE ridge, note

Freigerscharte

Becher Hut (on far side
of Übeltal glacier
E branch)

3025

of summit. Here climb the fairly steep snow/ice slope (small bergschrund possible) to a point a few m L of summit cross (1h).

South-West Ridge. A good sound rock ridge with only occasional loose stuff. II. An interesting way to summit from the Pfaffennieder.

87 It is possible to turn the first hump by going via Müller hut and joining ridge at pt.3228; otherwise take it more or less direct, including the largest tower. Minor deviations can be made L or R and later one can use snow R to save time. So reach the NW ridge (R.88) where a clear path develops with plentiful red marks and some fixed ropes; now easily to the top (2-2h30).

North-West Ridge. Approached from the Sulzenau hut over the Fernerstube, a good route of exposed scrambling following the glacier trek. F+.

88 From Sulzenau hut take R.38 to the Fernerstube. Keep N of the glacier and loop S after passing c2900m prior to an ENE course after c3060m to attain the NW ridge at a col pt.3144 - Lübecke Scharte, not named on AV map. Follow the ridge (II) to join the SW ridge, then to the top (4h).

North Flank Route. An interesting glacier climb infrequently done in summer (though often on ski) with quite complex crevasse work. Interest is somewhat diminished by stonefall danger at the tongue of the glacier. PD.

89 From Sulzenau hut take R.85b towards the Grünausee. Instead of following the moraine path up to the lake, keep R towards the steep narrow tongue of the Wilder Freiger Ferner. Climb this (stonefall), keeping R(W) of centre; when the gradient eases move up to a rock spur in middle of the glacier c2640m. Now keep just L(E) of the spur, steering among crevasses a little E of S towards pt.3324. In doing this it can be easier to sweep E above 2900m before returning to centre of this branch of the glacier to reach pt.3324, thereafter joining the Ordinary route (5h from hut).

The alternative W branch route, aiming for foot of the Wilder Freiger N ridge, is steeper and a little more difficult. It ends by turning the N ridge L(E) and climbing easy snow to top.

South-East Ridge. Runs from the Freigerscharte (3025m) and is a little used ascent route over pt.3157 and pt.3194 to pt.3313. After this merely on snow and sometimes rocks to the Signalgipfel and the summit. F (I+) (1h30).

Note: The Freigerscharte is reached in about 2h30 from the Nürnberger hut up the Grüblferner or alternatively in one h. or so from the Becherhaus after descending NE from hut and contouring round the glacier c3000m. For the normal route from the Becherhaus, see R.8.

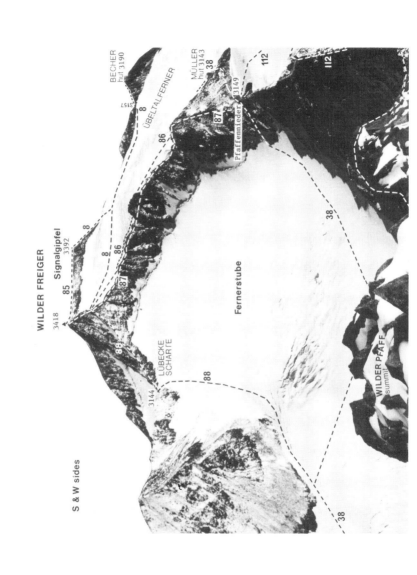

WILDER FREIGER

S & W sides

BECHER hut 3190

ÜBELTALFERNER

MÜLLER hut 3143

Signalgipfel 3392

3157

3418

3144

Pfaffennieder 3149

Fernerstube

LÜBECKE SCHARTE

WILDER PFAFF summit

85

8

8

8

86

86

87

87

88

88

88

87

38

38

38

112

112

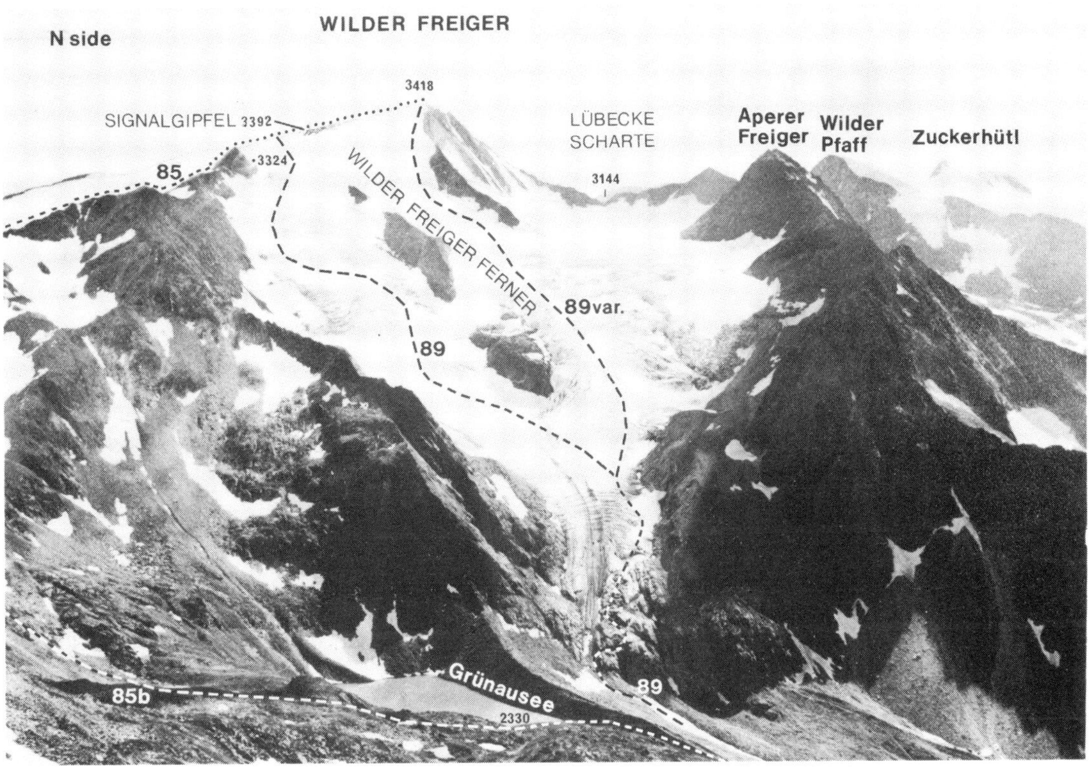

N side   WILDER FREIGER

Aperer Wilder Zuckerhütl
Freiger Pfaff

LÜBECKE
SCHARTE
3144

89 var.

WILDER FREIGER FERNER

89

3418

SIGNALGIPFEL 3392

3324

85

85b

Grünausee

2330

APERER FREIGER   3262m   **SULZENAUKOGEL**   2947m

Two unimportant summits on the ridge from Wilder Freiger that describes almost a semi-circle concave E and divides the Fernerstube from the Wilder Freiger Ferner. Loose rocks and scree are the only significant features.

GAMSSPITZL   3052m   **URFALLSPITZE**   2808m

Two minor peaks on ridge running NNE from the Wilder Freiger Signalgipfel. Both can be climbed in 45 min. from the Seescharte (R.85). The Gamsspitzl is easy from this direction and can also be climbed from the S as an easy minor detour from the normal Wilder Freiger route at the point where it attains the crest close to pt.3127.

The Urfallspitze by its SW ridge from the Seescharte is II. If approached via its NW ridge from Niederl (see R.41a) it is more difficult (III in places), keeping on the ridge and including the traverse of 3 teeth between the col at pt.2688 and 2698 (2h).

MAIRSPITZE   2781m

Last peak on the Wilder Freiger NNE ridge. Easily bagged from the Sulzenau-Nürnberger hut connecting path (R.41b) in 15 min.

ROTER GRAT   3099m   **HOCHGRINTL**   3033m
HOHE WAND   2973m

3 unimportant peaks at head of the Grüblferner W branch. Can be traversed without difficulty from the Freigerscharte to the Enges Türl in 2h30-3h. Reckon on 2h30 to either saddle from Nürnberger hut. Hochgrintl can be climbed from both N and S directly - but with little point.

ENGES TÜRL is the westernmost col along this ridge and can be climbed without difficulty from either side, though quite steep on the N. **WEITES TÜRL** is the easternmost and though easy on S side is rather more difficult, icy and steep on the N.

GEISSWANDSPITZE   2970m

A peak of little interest on the southern aspect of the small Geisswandferner. Easily climbed from the Rotgratscharte over a flattish saddle pt.2903 in 35 min.

FEUERSTEIN   ÖST. 3268m   WEST. 3245m

Prominent peaks with pleasant ascent routes and commanding fine views. About equidistant from Bremer and Nürnberger

82

FEUERSTEINE

Östl. Westl.
3268 3245

96
53
3105
VAR (90)
Magdeburger Scharte
90

90

90b

Grüblferner

Nürnberger Scharte

from NW

huts.   The most rewarding expedition is a traverse of both
peaks and descent by W ridge of the W peak, but even an
isolated visit to the E top is worthwhile and straightforward.

Feuersteine Traverse.   E to W peaks, PD.   FA.   P.Koller and
H.Loschge, 1881.

90   (a)   From Bremer hut reverse R.14 to the Simmingjöchl
(1h).   Turn S over rocks, traces of path, to the Aperer
Feuerstein Ferner and climb easily to the Nürnberger Scharte.
(b)   From Nürnberger hut take the Simmingjöchl path
(R.14) until it crosses the stream coming down from the
Grüblferner.   Go up L of stream and soon cross over the
moraine bank, usually onto snow.   Turn SE to keep pt.2585
and pt.2627 to your R.   Round a rocky promontory S and
soon after passing c2700m turn N and, winding first L then
R, take the best line onto the snowfield (occasional cairns)
SW of the Nürnberger Scharte (2914m), passing between pt.
2852 and 2920.   This line is clearly indicated on AV map.

From the Nürnberger Scharte head SE up easy snow slopes,
keeping to R of the rock ridge running up to the Pflerscher
Hochjoch.   (Note: From the Bremer hut a shortcut for experienced parties in good snow conditions follows the W side
of the W branch of the Simmingferner to the small depression
pt.3026.   It saves about 30 min.).   Now either (i) cross the
snow slope S to join the NW ridge of the E peak, adjusting
direction slightly if necessary to overcome the usually easy
bergschrund.   Follow ridge, rocks or sometimes mostly snow,
easily to top (3-3h30).   Or (ii) continue SE to the Pflerscher
Hochjoch, then climb mainly on the snowy R side of the NE
ridge to E summit (30 min. longer).

The traverse to W peak is easy.   Go down SW to a col, some
loose rocks, turning a few rock teeth R, and climb the ensuing
ridge or snow R to the top (30 min.).   Now more difficult, go
down jagged W ridge to the Weites Türl saddle (2840m), keeping to crest over most of the pinnacles (II/II+), but turning
the last ones L(S) (1h30).   The descent from saddle onto the
Grüblferner can be awkward; first a few broken rocks, then
a steep snow/ice slope to the glacier basin.   Finally cross the
glacier N, keeping L of pt.2627 and 2585 to join the outward
route at c2400 (6-8h for traverse).

The W peak can also be climbed by its S ridge from the Magdeburger Scharte (R.53) (II) in 45 min.   Only occasional deviations to the W are required.   A good route, also that of the
FA. by J.Ficker, F.Gleinser, L.Purtscheller, 1869.

PFLERSCHER HOCHJOCH   3166m

Difficult to recognise as a peak in its own right from some
angles, appearing only as a corner point at the E extremity of
the Grüblferner.   Rarely climbed for itself but easy from the

Nürnberger Scharte. For this and the connection with the Östl. Feuerstein see R.90. From the Pflerscher Niederjoch at its E foot it is 30 min. over mixed snow and rocks (I).

From North. What used to be a pleasant climb up steep glac-ier slopes has become less interesting because of the recession now causing a tiresome initial moraine plod. Nevertheless it might still be used as an interesting approach to Feuersteine.

91   From Bremer hut follow the Simmingjöchl path (R.14) for 15 min. until it starts to gain height, then drop down slightly onto the Simmingferner moraine. Head SSW up the W branch to c2600m at the foot of rocks that drop N from the summit. Turn the lowest rocks R(N) and climb the steep snow slope, passing just R of pt.2872. However the glacier is deteriora-ting here and you may need to make a diversion R. Then keep due S to reach the peak's ill-defined NW ridge at 3110m. Go SE up a gentle snow slope (or the crest and a few rocks) to the top (3h).

SCHNEESPITZ (SCHNEEPINGGL)   3178m

Snow dome with a rock crest and some good climbs. It can be combined with the Pflerscher Hochjoch and the Feuersteine. Seen at its best from the vicinity of the Bremer hut.

Traverse from Pflerscher Hochjoch. Normal route from Bremer and Nürnberger huts, PD. FA. Dr L.Scholz, F.Pfurtscheller, 1886.

92   As for R.90 or R.91 to the Pflerscher Hochjoch. Descend its mixed E ridge or keep L of crest on snow to the Pflerscher Niederjoch (large cairn) and reach the Schneespitz by its W ridge which has some steep but straightforward rock to negot-iate (III) (1h from Pflerscher Hochjoch, 4-5h from Bremer or Nürnberger huts).

South-East Ridge. One of the 2 straightforward approaches from the Magdeburger hut, F. FA. F.Pfurtscheller, L.Scholz, 1886.

93   From Magdeburger hut follow the Stubenferner path (R.53) amost to the Sudl. Stuben Scharte, where the route for the Feuersteinferner and Magdeburger Scharte breaks off L. From here continue W to foot of the SE ridge, then along the short ridge (I) to summit (3h).

South-East Flank. Alternative way from Magdeburger hut. F. FA. J.Ficker, J.Kuen, J.Markart, 1871.

94   Follow R.53 towards the Südl. Stuben Scharte. Fork R in 25 min. at a signed junction, c2600m. The marked way over boulders and snow patches is difficult to follow. Aim to cross the glacier debris at c2650m, heading N towards the frontier

N side

Schneespitze
3178

Pflerscher
Niederjoch
3065

Pflerscher
Hochjoch
3166

Östl.
Feuerstein
3268

NÜRNBERGER
SCHARTE
2914

Simmingjöchl
2761

SIMMINGFERNER

92 · 92 · 92 · 90var. · 90 · 91 · 90a · 95 · 91 · 14

ridge. A little higher, where the glacier proper starts, turn W into the N arm of the Stubenferner and climb steeply towards the Nördl. Stuben (Bremer) Scharte. A plateau thereabouts leads to another steeper snow slope, then to gentler inclines of snow and rocks of the summit dome (2h30 from hut). Note: in poor visibility the summit itself may be hard to find. Another way to the top from the Nördl. Stuben Scharte, keeping to the ridge, is straightforward (I+) with occasional gendarmes avoidable L, returning to the snowfield at c3100m.

A traverse of the Schneespitz, Pflerscher Hochjoch and Östl. Feuerstein makes an outstanding day from Magdeburger hut to either Bremer or Nürnberger huts and is highly recommended, PD (6-8h).

North Face. A good ice climb though it can present considerable crevasse problems and stonefall danger especially late in the season. The glacier has receded enormously over the last decade. AD.

95 Leave the Bremer hut on the Simmingjöchl track and descend onto the Simmingferner. Climb the glacier keeping to E side of the E branch and L of crevasses. At this pt. a rocky mass topped by a hanging glacier lies between you and the summit. On its L a steep snow/ice gully (Mühlsteiger Couloir) is no longer recommended as a way to upper snowfield of the Simmingferner. The bergschrund at the bottom is often hard, sometimes impossible and there is considerable stonefall danger. The usual way now from c2760m keeps R round the rocky mass and continues up crevassed slopes to the Pflerscher Niederjoch pt.3065 with only the short steep mixed ridge to finish. However this route may also pose some thoughtful moments because of the crevasses (3h30 from hut; longer if crevasses force significant diversions).

AGGLSSPITZE   3196m

Small peak, snow covered almost to ridge on the E side.

North-West Ridge. Straightforward peak-bagging opportunity from the Magdeburger Scharte, F. FA. D.Diamantidi, P.Koller, 1890.

96 Reach Magdeburger Scharte from Teplitzer or Magdeburger huts by R.53, or feasibly but rarely via the Westl. Feuerstein S ridge. From col go SE over snow, then more steeply over rocks without difficulty to a forepeak. A gendarme near the top can be turned high and L or lower and much easier to R (45 min.).

From Teplitzer hut. Rather tortuous but unusual and worth combining with R.96 as a round trip.

97 Reverse R.53 to pt.2830. From here a path leads SE into an area called Hoher Trog (ever so Lake District, literally Higher Trough) to foot of a spiky ridge coming down from the Rochollspitze. This path numbered 9A continues on to the Pfurnsee, then down to Agglsboden. Keep W of this, aiming for small col pt.3046 to attain the Agglsspitze SE ridge. It takes 30 min. from here, staying on the ridge (II).

ROCHOLLSPITZE   3081m

Small rock peak above the Feuersteinferner usually climbed from the Magdeburger hut and often combined with the Agglsspitze, without difficulty either from the col pt.3046 on its NW ridge (I) in 10 min., or by turning S at c2900m on the Feuerstein-ferner to join the E ridge. This latter option takes about 2h30 from hut and, if you are doing the Agglsspitze as well, saves retracing your steps.

ZWERCHWAND   2934m

Though pt.2934 is the highest pt. the name is correctly applied to the whole N-S ridge. The steep E wall falls into the area called "In dem Flecken". On the W side the ridge is easily att-ained from the Feuersteinferner. On ÖK 2710 the highest pt. is incorrectly labelled Lorenzspitze. The mountain can be climbed by the easy NW ridge from the Agglsjoch pt.2836 in 30 min. or, if approaching from the Magdeburger hut (see R.97), cutting the corner on the Feuersteinferner to go up to the NE ridge, F (2h). The W flank is very loose. Traverse SE to the Lorenz-spitze is III.

AGGLSJOCH (2836m) is, as the name tells, not a peak but a pass and a little-used one at that. Nevertheless a potentially handy and unusual connection from the Pflerschtal into the Rid-nauntal; the Zwerchwand is easy to bag en route. F.

98   Leave the Pflerschtal-Magdeburger hut path (R.36) at c2040m where it turns sharply E away from the stream. Both the AV map and ÖK 2710 indicate a small path here but only traces remain to begin with and the stream crossing pt. is vague. A broader track later appears and goes down to the Ferner stream. Note that the Grünsee marked on AV map no longer exists and is merely a marshy meadow. This area can also be reached more easily though without the earlier benefit of a good path by staying on S bank of the Pflersch stream and following it up to the indicated site of the lake. Now follow the Ferner stream generally W over boulders and up onto the Feuerstein-ferner, thence SW to the pass (4-4h30). On the other side go down steeply SW over scree and rocks to N end of the Pfurn-see, then follow path No.9A in the same line to the Oberer Aggls Alm and down onto the Maiern-Grohmann hut track (R.5).

LORENZSPITZE   2886m

A rock peak climbed infrequently because of the miserable approach routes after end of July.   FA. F.Frech, R.H.Schmitt,1892.

99   Ascent from Pflerschtal.   Follow R.98 to site of the now
non-existent Grünsee.   From here climb SW steeply over grass
by a waterfall, rising to a more rocky area and later to a mess
of boulders which becomes most unpleasant.   The SW-leading
stream is a good landmark as is the obvious rocky promontory
pt.2602.   It is easier to round this latter pt. S, keeping on any
snow patches as much as possible; finally go SW up to the deep-
est pt. between Lorenzspitze and Ridnauner Schneespitz, a gap
pt.2803.   From here the ridge NW to the peak is II in places
and goes over pt.2818 with one short descent en route (4h30).
Except in good snow there is nothing on this ridge SE of the
Lorenzspitze which is worth the misery of getting up to it and
down again.

The SE ridge of the Lorenzspitze falls gradually away in height
and forms the boundary between the Pflerschtal and Ridnauntal.
It has a number of unimportant summits, all of which can be
ascended by at most a scramble.   These are **Ridnauner Schneespitze** (2860m),   **Hochtrogspitze** (2842m) - lies NE of the Áuss.
Hochegg rather than on the main ridge,   **Áusseres Hochegg**
(2880m) - called Hocheck on ÖK 2710,   **Winkeljochspitze** (2810m),
Ellesspitze (2661m),   **Maurerspitze** (2628m),   **Maratschspitze**
(2648m) - lies NE of the Maurerspitze,   **Wetterspitze** (2709m).

There is a good connection (Path No.27) from Innerpflersch
to Maiern and Inn. Ridnaun, running up past Allriss Alm and
along W bank of the Allriss stream, to cross the ridge at the
Maurer Scharte between the Maurerspitze and the Wetterspitze.

Section 4 WESTERN HAUPTKAMM

WÜTENKARSATTEL AND WINDACHER DAUNKOGEL TO THE WILDERPFAFF – INCLUDING ASSOCIATED PEAKS NORTHWARDS TO THE NÖRDL. DAUNKOGEL

WINDACHER DAUNKOGEL   3351m

Fine mountain dominating head of the Sulztal. The easiest way up (I) is via the unimaginative S face over boulders from the Warenkarscharte (40 min.). The short N face is a steep climb on unpleasant outward sloping rocks, stonefall danger, III.

West Ridge. An attractive ridge of snow and rocks, F/PD depending on conditions. FA. F.Jennewein, H.Buchner, 1876.

100 (a) From the Hochstubai hut descend 100m NE over upper basin of the Wütenkarferner and contour NW before ascending a scree slope to the Wütenkarsattel (3115m) (30 min.).
      (b) From the Dresdner hut follow R.33a to the Daunscharte (alternatively R.33b from Eisgrat station on the Stubai Gletscherbahn) and onward to the Wütenkarsattel (3h30, shorter from Eisgrat).
      (c) From the Amberger hut follow R.32 to the Wütenkarsattel (3h30).

From the saddle go ESE up a snow slope and loose rocks to the lower top (3301m). Scramble along rock ridge to a snow crest which is followed to the summit rocks. The narrow section of this crest is often corniced early in the season (45 min. from the saddle).

101 East Ridge - traverse from Westl. Daunkogel, an interesting excursion despite some loose rock, PD. From the Westl. summit (see R.102,103) descend the rock ridge WSW towards c3260m, the lowest pt. between the Westl. and Windacher Daunkogel. Shortly before this depression turn a fine pinnacle on the R. Follow broad snow crest and climb the rock ridge, traversing 2 knolls, to summit (1h30 from Westl. Daunkogel).

WARENKARSEITENSPITZE   3345m

First peak on the subsidiary ridge running initially S from the Windacher Daunkogel then bending W. It lies just SW of the Warenkarscharte from which it can be climbed with no difficulty in 45 min. (I). The S and W ridges also offer possibilities (II) but the rock is poor.

Wildkarspitze 3173m   The Hochstubaihütte is situated on this insignificant hump.   **Hoher Nebelkogel** 3211m   A 15 min. scramble from the Hochstubai hut.

WINDACHER DAUNKOGEL   N side

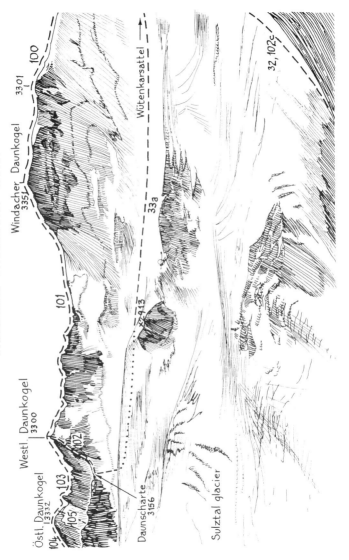

Östl. Daunkogel 13332
104
103
105
Westl. Daunkogel 3300
102
101
Daunscharte 3156
Sulztal glacier
27,913
33a
Wütenkarsattel
Windacher Daunkogel 3351
100
3301
32, 102c

WESTLICHE DAUNKOGEL   3300m

Attractive triangular mountain at the pt. where the Daunkogel-
kamm turns N. Not often climbed for its own sake.

North Ridge. Ordinary route, F. Although the approaches go
through fine scenery this is an unexciting finale. FA. F.Drasch,
L.Purtscheller, 1887.

102 (a) From Dresdner hut by R.33a to the Daunscharte.
     (b) From Hochstubai hut reverse R.32 to Wütenkarsattel,
then reverse R.33a, climbing the steep snow/ice slope to the
Daunscharte.
     (c) From Amberger hut take R.32 as far as c2900m on the
Sulztalferner, then veering SE to join R.102b.

From the Daunscharte climb broken rocks and scree of the broad
N ridge without difficulty to top in 30 min. (3h from Dresdner,
2h30 from Hochstubai, 4h from Amberger).

South-East Ridge from Östl. Daunkogel. The most interesting
way, predominantly rock, PD+. FA. A.Pallocsay, J.Kindl, 1888.

103 From the Östl. Daunkogel descend easy rocks to the snow
crest above the N face. Go along it then traverse a sharp
knoll (II). Continue slightly downwards on the serrated crest
until the ridge steepens and offers short slabby pitches (II/III),
easing off a little before the summit (1h30)

For the W ridge from the Windacher Daunkogel, see R.101.

Ridge between Daunscharte and Daunjoch

Several small summits (highest 3184m) occur on this N-running
ridge some 1.5 km long. Loose rock in places, rope not essential though might be preferred because of momentary exposure.
Uninteresting climbing but superb views and can be combined
with one or more of the Daunkogel summits to make an interesting round day-trip from the Dresdner hut or from the valley, I.
Allow 1-1h30 for the ridge itself.

Hinterer Daunkopf 3225m   Undistinguished mountain usually
climbed only as a digression by those crossing the Daunjoch;
see Amberger-Dresdner hut connection, R.2. From Daunjoch
simply push up through loose rocks of the S ridge in 30 min.
(I). Or from Amberger hut use a long glacier tongue rising
S from the cirque that lies just W of the Nördl. Daunkogel –
this is better than the Daunjoch way.

Nördliche Daunkogel 3076m   Unimportant peak S of the Mutterberger Joch. Hardly ever climbed. From the Joch in 15 min.
by short N ridge which can be turned at will on E side. The
connecting ridge from the Hinterer Daunkopf has some jagged
sections, III (2-3h).

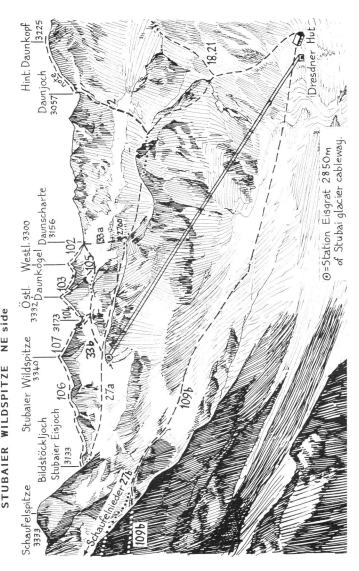

STUBAIER WILDSPITZE NE side

Schaufelspitze 3333
Bildstöckljoch
Stubaier Eisjoch 3133
Stubaler Wildspitze 3340
Stubaler Wildspitze
Östl. 3332 Daunkögel
Westl. 3300 Daunkögel
Daunscharte 3156
Daunjoch 3057
Hint. Daunkopf 3225

Schaufelnieder 27b

⊙ = Station Eisgrat 2850 m
of Stubai glacier cableway.

Dresdner Hut

ÖSTLICHE DAUNKOGEL   3332m

Interesting summit with some good climbs to suit all tastes.
Often combined with a traverse of the Stubaier Wildspitze. A
traverse of the whole Hauptkamm from the Wildspitze to the
Windacher Daunkogel is a superb expedition, AD if you stick to
the ridge. Using the Gletscherbahn to the Eisgrat station and
quickly walking to the Eisjoch (R.27a) gives a rapid start for
the 7h+ time required for the whole traverse, finishing at the
Hochstubai hut. Purists might prefer to begin at the Hildesheimer hut which will take a little longer.

104   South-East Ridge. Ordinary route, F. FA. A.Pallocsay,
J.Kindl, 1888.
(a)   From Dresdner hut take R.27a towards the Eisgrat, moving
R onto the glacier just before passing 2700m. Go SW onto the
Daunkogelferner, keeping rock island pt.2992 on your L side.
Then SSW and later SW to pt.3173 (2h30).
(b)   From Eisgrat station go WSW gently up the glacier, passing just S of rock island pt.3013 and gradually turning SW to
reach pt.3173 (crevasses), the saddle at foot of SE ridge (1h).

Turn an obvious rock step on R and climb steep ridge to top,
II (30 min.).

105   North Face. A short steep ice climb of similar standard
to Ruderhofspitze N face, 160m, AD-. From Dresdner hut take
R.33a for the Daunscharte but climb the glacier SW to intersect
with R.33b thereby climbing above a crevassed area. At c3140m
head S to foot of the face. Cross bergschrund and climb the
plain slope of 50/55° to the W ridge. Scramble easy rocks to
the summit (3h30-4h from hut).
Starting from the Eisgrat station as for R.33b makes it much shorter
and avoids the despoiled and boulder-strewn slopes lower down.

STUBAIER WILDSPITZE   3340m

Fine pointed peak, usually traversed; an easy day if the Gletscherbahn is used. FA. E.Fuchs, L.Purtscheller, K.Egger, 1881.

106   South-East Ridge. PD-, mostly II, one pitch III+. FA.
M.Leigh-Clare, M.Schweizer, 1890.
(a)   From Dresdner hut (or Eisgrat station) reach the Eisjoch
by R.27a (2h30 or 30 min. respectively).
(b)   From Hildesheimer hut reverse R.27a to same point. Move
NW along track just N of the col (danger from skiers when you
cross the piste) and move to R of the small lake and over boulders with snow patches up onto the broad ridge. At pt.3193
the ridge narrows abruptly. Go along it to rocky hump pt.3255
and descend a little to pt.3235. Continue up the pleasant ridge
on largely sound rock to top (1h30, 2h from Eisgrat, 3h from
Hildesheimer, 4h from Dresdner).

PFAFFENSCHNEIDE W side

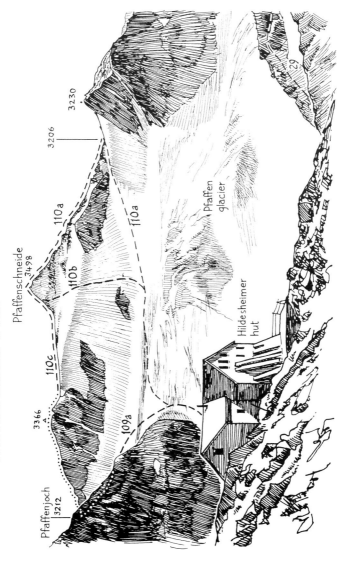

Pfaffenjoch 3212

3366

110c

110b

Pfaffenschneide 3498

110a

109a

110a

3230

3206

Pfaffen glacier

Hildesheimer hut

107 North-West Ridge. PD-. The first part from pt.3173 (the nameless saddle between Stubaier Wildspitze and Östl. Daunkogel) is III on sound rock, but it can be avoided for easier climbing further on. FA. A.Pallocsay, J.Kindl, 1888.

From Dresdner hut follow R.105 until just below pt.3173 but do not go up to the saddle. Instead turn the first prominent step of NW ridge on the L(N) and climb a gully to the ridge which then leads without difficulty to top (3h from hut).

Routes on the NE and N walls (III+/IV) are poor and scrappy.

South-East Flank. Mentioned as it is the ordinary route and much frequented by guided parties. Loose rock and uninteresting, F. Danger from stonefall, particularly from parties on the much better SE ridge above.

SCHAUFELSPITZE   3333m

Broad rocky summit, steep on N side and more gentle slopes to the S. When seen from Mutterbergalm, prominent and spectacular, but closer inspection is less flattering. Climbed frequently all year round but in truth worthy only as a viewpoint. The original way is the rather loose SW side from the Schaufelnieder.

108 South-West Flank. The only worthwhile way, scrappy, F.
(a) From Dresdner hut (or Eisgrat station) follow R.27a to the Stubaier Eisjoch (3133m). On the other side of the pass continue on the same route, contouring round to pt.3149, then turn NE towards the Isidornieder (3158m). Just before this small saddle scramble NE over loose rocks and scree, traces of path, keeping under the SW ridge to top (about 1h from the Eisjoch).
(b) From Hildesheimer hut reverse R.27a to pt.3149 and proceed as above (1h30).

Peilspitze 2820m   20 min. scramble from the Peiljoch (I). Aim for W ridge and follow to top. **Grosser Trögler** 2902m   Fine viewpoint, recommended as an alternative route for the transfer from Sulzenau to Dresdner huts. See R.19. **Aperer Pfaff** 3351m   Lies NW of the Pfaffenjoch and is of no real interest to climbers. The Aperer Pfaffengrat runs NE to the Peiljoch and is an important landmark crossed near the Lange Pfaffennieder on the normal route from the Dresdner hut to Zuckerhütl.

ZUCKERHÜTL   3505m

In older texts and still locally sometimes called **Zuckerhut**. It means "Sugar-hat" or better, "Sugarloaf". The highest point rises only 180m above the beautiful Sulzenauferner to the N, while the rocky S flank falls steeply to the Triebenkarlasferner. The ordinary glacier route is usually an easy snow tramp though late in season the upper few m of the normal E ridge can be icy with rocks exposed. Accidents, some fatal, are not uncommon here in such conditions and can be related to a failure to observe proper mountaineering techniques for the conditions. There is a particularly worrying disinclination to wear crampons. An enjoyable mountain notwithstanding its popularity and often crowded summit as the highest top in the Stubai Alps; spectacular views.

East Ridge. Ordinary route. FA. J.A.Specht with A.Tanzer, 1863. Appropriate to a very popular climb, can be done from the Hildesheimer, Dresdner, Sulzenau and, via Wilder Pfaff, the Müller huts. Now most frequently done as a "Tagestour" (day-trip) from the Stubaital using the Gletscherbahn to the Eisgrat station, or as a "Dreigipfel" tour from the Hildesheimer hut and taking in Wilder Pfaff and Wilder Freiger to finish at Nürnberger or Sulzenau huts. All approaches converge before or at the Pfaffensattel, the depression between Wilder Pfaff and Zucker-hütl. F.

109 (a) From Hildesheimer hut take path going NE down scree or snow past the small lake and continuing in the same line down a rockband – some exposure, fixed ropes. Continue E on a stony track with snow patches, subsequently ascending N bank of glacier keeping close to rocks of the Aperer Pfaff W ridge to the Pfaffen-joch (3212m) (1h). Cross the fairly level upper slopes of the Sulzenauferner (crevasses in line of march) to the Pfaffensattel (45 min.). Climb the snowy E ridge to summit cross; it steepens considerably towards the top (30 min., 2h30 from hut).

(b) From Dresdner hut follow R.27b to just beyond pt. 2808 (wrong as 2608 on AV map). At c2800m turn E across the glacier to the Lange Pfaffennieder (3055m), a slight depression in the long Aperer Pfaffengrat that separates the Fernau and Sulzenau glaciers. A steep scree and rock slope leads up the final 100m distance towards the gap. Go up to within a few m of the crest, then scramble up R to reach the ridge a little above the lowest pt. (2h). Continue along the rocky Aperer Pfaff ridge just L (E) of crest up to c3120m then go S over rocks and snow, including one large permanent snow patch, without losing height onto the Sulzenauferner. (Note: It is tempting, indeed often suggested by footmarks and scratched rocks, to go straight over the Aperer Pfaffengrat down to the Sulzenauferner. If you then continue across the glacier to "cut the corner" it can involve moderately complex crevasse work). Keep S along W side of the glacier to 3200m, veering SE to join the Pfaffen-joch – Pfaffensattel route at c3250m (45 min.).

(c) From the Eisgrat station cross the Schaufelferner E (crevasses), descending slightly to round the obvious rocky pro-montory at c2800m before crossing the Fernauferner E to join (b) just below the Lange Pfaffennieder.

(d) From Sulzenau hut follow R.30 to join (b) and (c) above. Above c2950m the same warning note applies as in (a).

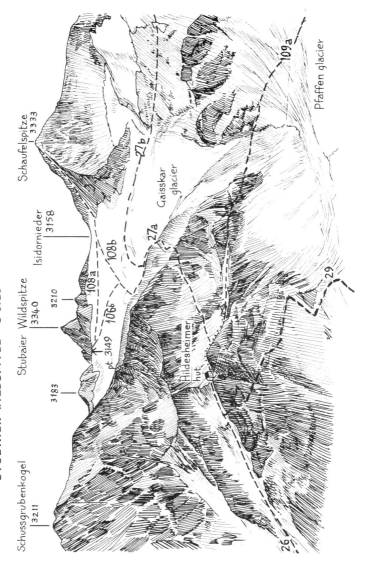

STUBAIER WILDSPITZE   S side

Schussgrubenkogel
3211

Stubaier Wildspitze
3340

Isidornieder
3158

Schaufelspitze
3333

3183

3210

pt. 3149

108a

108b

106b

27a

27b

Gaisskar glacier

109a

Pfaffen glacier

Hildesheimer hut

26

29

West Ridge from the Pfaffenschneide, pt.3498.   An interesting
alternative to the ordinary route, straightforward in good conditions and only 30 min. longer, F+. FA (of Pfaffenschneide):
L.Pfaundler, L.von Barth, 1862.

110   There are 3 options.   The first 2 are only really applic-
able to those approaching from the Hildesheimer hut.
     (a)   Cut across the Pfaffenferner SE from c3040m to join the
Pfaffenschneide SW ridge at a saddle pt.3206, thereafter following ridge easily to summit.
     (b)   From the same height on the Pfaffenferner head for the
obvious rock island on W slope of the mountain at c3140m and
take steep snow towards the summit ridge.
     (c)   From the other huts or from the Hildesheimer go up to
the Pfaffenjoch then turn SSE and subsequently S, keeping pt.
3366 to R, and finally ascend a steep snow slope to summit ridge
(2h from Hildesheimer, 3h+ from Dresdner, 4h30 from Sulzenau).

From Siegerland hut the mountain can be climbed by taking the
Hildesheimer track (R.29) to the cirque below and E of the Geisskogel, subsequently ascending steep scree and rocks to join the
Pfaffenschneide SW ridge at pt.3230 and continuing as above -
quite easy but long and obviously circuitous.

From the Pfaffenschneide descend snowy E ridge towards pt.3432,
the lowest pt. between Pfaffenschneide and Zuckerhütl, moving
L and down on snow to round the gap before climbing quite
steeply on snow towards the summit cross (45 min.).

North Face.   An attractive snow/ice face, 160m, 55° at mid-height,
AD-.   **South Face.**   III, one pitch IV, objectively dangerous
from stonefall.   Starts on the Triebenkarlasferner below the summit at an obvious tongue of ice.   Strictly for heroes.

WILDER PFAFF   3458m
Wild Priest.   Gentle snow slopes on NW side belie the name though
it has a steep and mostly rocky wild NE face.   Usually combined
with Zuckerhütl.

111 Ordinary Route.   F.   FA. A.Gutberlet, L.Purtscheller,
A.Tanzer, 1870.   Reach the Pfaffensattel by R.109 and go up
snow slope L (N) of the W ridge to the large summit (20 min.).

112 East Ridge.   Easy, entertaining scramble; old fixed ropes
over a slab near the top.   After fresh snow it is much trickier, F.
From Müller hut go WNW over boulders and usually snow patches
to the Pfaffennieder (3149m).   The E ridge begins here but it is
usual to make a sweep S on a snow bank round a small glacier
pool to attain the ridge higher up and close to pt.3270.   Follow
steepening ridge to summit (1h30 from hut).

WILDER PFAFF – ZUCKERHÜTL N side

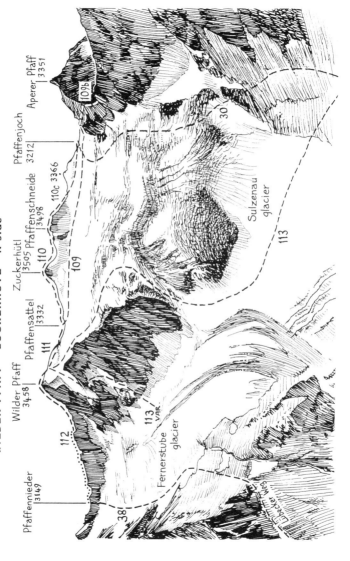

Aperer Pfaff 3351

Pfaffenjoch

Pfaffenschneide 3212

110c 3366

Pfaffenschneide 3498

Zuckerhütl 3505

Pfaffensattel 3332

Wilder Pfaff 3458

Pfaffennieder 3149

109b

30

Sulzenau glacier

113

111

110

109

113 var.

112

Fernerstube glacier

38

Lübecker Weg

113 From North. AD.   FA. H.Hess, L.Purtscheller, 1887.
From Sulzenau hut follow the Peiljoch track (R.19), continuing
along the moraine until it is easy to get onto the glacier above
the lower crevassed area. Then move SE under the dramatic
icefall – keep your distance from it and show caution, falling
debris – increasingly steeply to foot of the rocky N ridge which
separates the Sulzenauferner and the Fernerstube. Just W of
the ridge foot a steep band of snow/ice leads up through the
crevasses. Higher, continue up the ridge until you can move on
snow to the top (4h30-5h from hut).

More direct snow/ice/rock N wall routes are much beset by stonefall and not generally recommended. In good ice conditions there
is a small local following for a fairly direct approach to summit from
the Fernerstube. This route is indicated on photograph.

South Ridge. From the Sonklarscharte pt.3298 (not named on AV
map), easily reached from the Übeltalferner, poor rock, III, not a
good route.

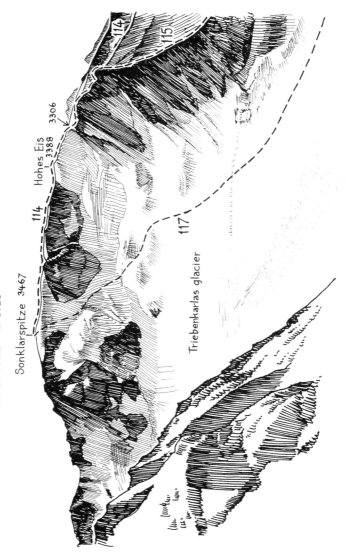

SONKLARSPITZE W side

Sonklarspitze 3467

114

Hohes Eis
3388
3306

114

115

117

Triebenkarlas glacier

Section 5 WINDACHKAMM

From the Brenner pass the frontier ridge coincides with the Haupt-kamm as far as Wilder Pfaff, a topographically important pt. Here the frontier changes direction and runs S over the Sonklarspitze to the Schwarzwandspitze where the ridge divides. The SW (later W) branch forms the Windachkamm as well as the frontier ridge, the SE branch the Botzerkamm (Section 6). Strictly speaking the Sonklarspitze and Schwarzwandspitze do not belong to the Windach-kamm but for reasons of convenience they are included in this part with other climbs connected with the Siegerland hut.

SONKLARSPITZE   3467m

Large snow dome summit with a splendid southern view of the front-ier ridge. The most popular outing from the Siegerland hut. The Übeltalferner on the Ital. (E) side is the largest glacier in the Stubai.   FA. R.Gutberlet with A.Tanzer, S.Holzmann, 1869 - by the loose N ridge from the Sonklarscharte (unnamed on AV map); after getting onto ridge from the Übeltalferner go W round first step and return to ridge using a steep gully.

South-West Ordinary Route. F. FA. W. & O.Chiari, E. von Böhm, P. Kotter, 1878.

114   From Siegerland hut ascend NNE to the small glacier - hardly any snow in late season - between the Scheiblehnwand and SW ridge of Hohes Eis, aiming for a couloir in top R-hand corner. Considerable summer stonefall here, so it is better to go R just before the couloir as shown on AV map to an obvious small saddle in the rocky ridge (red paint flashes). Keep on ridge towards Hohes Eis, to another small col with a 5m rock step. A fixed rope goes steeply down L to turn the step. Then pass pt.3306 and keep R (E) along the quite sharp snow crest. After Hohes Eis (3388m) turn N over the trig. pt. and, keeping the steepness to your L, continue on snow to summit (2h30 from hut).

Hohes Eis W ridge by the Scheiblehnwand. A little longer than the ordinary route but more interesting, F+, a few pitches II. FA. R.Kaulich, E.Mayer, 1920.

115   From Siegerland hut take the Hildesheimer hut connecting path (R.29) to foot of the Scheiblehnwand. Climb rocks NE to the ridge then go along it over pt.2850, 3020 and 3182 to join R.114 at pt.3306 (2h30-3h from hut).

116 East Side approach. Marginally the shortest way to top, F+. From Müller hut head SSW to foot of the ill-defined E ridge - more of a spur. Move a little W (on N side of spur) and climb SW up

Hohes
SONKLARSPITZE Eis 3388
Wilder 3467
Pfaff
.3458

ZUCKERHÜTL
3505

Pfaffenschneide
3498

114

Siegerland
hut

29

Triebenkarlasferner
115

Gamsplatzl
3019

←Sölden

from S

steep snow then rocks until snow slopes lead WNW to top (say 2h).
Alternatively, start by first crossing to the Pfaffennieder.

117   West Face.   Little frequented but good ice climb, 250m, AD.
From Siegerland hut follow the Hildesheimer hut track (R.29) as
far as the Triebenkarlasferner.   Go up glacier towards the rocky
spur which projects W from the Wilder Pfaff-Sonklarspitze ridge
just N of the summit.   Now pick the best route through the icefall S of the spur to reach easier ground.   Above cross a bergschrund (often dificult late in season) and climb steeply again on
snow to finish just SW of the summit (3h).

SCHWARZWANDSPITZE   3358m

This peak constitutes the southernmost outpost of the Hauptkamm
where the ridge divides into the Windachkamm and Botzerkamm.
It lies at the N extremity of the long Schwarze Wand ridge and
is usually bagged before or after an ascent of the Sonklarspitze.
It is an easy plod from one summit to the other.   There are
several straightforward ascents and this permits some interesting round trips to be accomplished amidst beautiful scenery.

South-East Ridge.   An easy ascent from the Schwarzwandscharte,
I, 40 min.

118   From West.   F+.   From Siegerland hut go ENE up the remains of the Östl. Scheiblehnferner under the ridge joining Hohes
Eis and the Schwarzwandspitze.   What used to be a snow/ice
couloir rising to join the NW ridge just L (NW) of pt.3294 is now
more often a scree-filled runnel with snow bilaterally.   This
depends on the season and the snow.   Notwithstanding a tedious
approach from the bottom, this would make a better approach to
the Schwarze Wand than the even looser Windachscharte.   After
climbing the couloir on the L follow rather loose ridge to pt.
3294, then SE over snow to the summit (2h30).

119   Along the Schwarze Wand.   This solid granite ridge can be
undertaken in its entirety or in part as there is access at pt.
3062, a small col just NE of pt.3094.   Once a steep snowfield with
a bergschrund, this is now often only a miserable scree slope
above the remains of the Östl. Scheiblehnferner.   Glacier recession has made this ridge a much less attractive proposition
than it used to be.   I/II.
The ridge itself starts at the Windachscharte (2862m), a border
crossing pt. embracing a path through boulders and scree and
snow in early season, from the Siegerland hut to the pleasant
Schwarzsee above Timmelsalp (but see note on R.48).   Once on
the ridge, pass a col (2867m) and go up to pt.2903.   Then onwards without difficulty to pt.3094; latter pt. can also be reached more directly using its easy SW ridge.   Subsequently stay
on the crest.   After another col pt.3062 a large step can be

taken directly (II) or avoided L (W). 1h30 from Windachscharte
to pt.3094, another 1h+ to summit. Allow 45-60 min. from hut
to reach the Windachscharte.

Beillöcherspitze 3065m   Rocky peak at E end of the Windachkamm. The ridge from the Windachscharte is IV with several
gendarmes - the hardest 2 can be turned on Ital. side (2h30).

SCHEIBLEHNKOGEL   3060m

Pleasant peak climbed frequently from the Siegerland hut.   An
excellent viewpoint.   FA probably by Ludwig Purtscheller as
part of his traverse of the peaks S of the Windachtal in 1892.

120   WNW Flank. F-, very easy.   From hut descend the valley
track to c2620m then take a signposted fork L over a veritable
boulder jumble, guided by occasional red paint flashes.   The
route more or less contours the foot of the Scheiblehnkogel NW
ridge, getting onto the Westl. Scheiblehnferner at c2700m. Now
climb easy glacier, only a few small crevasses, by its eastern
edge, aiming for a gap pt.2888 on ridge E of the Hohlkogel.
From here a straightforward walk/scramble up the ridge or just
below it to the top (2h).

The NW ridge is II; the initial towers can be avoided on the R,
staying on the ridge and traversing some rock teeth to finish.
The short connecting ridge to the Beillöcherspitze is quite loose
and includes a slab pitch of II.
Traversing the ridge to the Hint. Kitzkogel in its entirety is not
difficult (see also R.121) but it is much simpler and just as nice
to use the glacier to turn the Hohlkogel, getting back onto the
ridge at pt.2916.

HINTERER KITZKOGEL   3063m

Agreeable as part of the Windachkamm traverse (R.123) or as a
shortish route from the Siegerland hut.   A traverse to the Scheiblehnkogel can make a more interesting circular trip, F+.

121   (a)   Follow R.120 to c2700m.   From here the best way is to
climb S up the glacier to a gap in the ridge at pt.2888, W of a
rocky hump that is the Hohlkogel.   Follow ridge on quite sound
rock (II) to a small col where a steep snow bay rises to meet
ridge just E of pt.3050.   This col can also be reached directly
from lower part of the glacier, finishing directly up the slope -
icy by late August and by then with a bergschrund which may
be large and difficult to cross.
At pt.3050, a cross and a summit book; this is not the top. The
true summit lies further NW along the ridge you are ascending.
In mist this is confusing.   Note that there are 2 westward leading ridges which enclose a small snowfield.   The top pt.3063 lies
close to the junction of N ridge of the mountain and the northernmost of the aforementioned W ridges (2h30).

(b)   Branch R, also waymarked, from R.120 just W of the small lake.   Continue W and round the N ridge of the Hinterer Kitzkogel before turning S.   Follow middle of the glacier and go up to W ridge close to summit.

Vorderer Kitzkogel 3060m   Interesting only as part of a traverse of the Windachkamm – see R.123.

Timmelsjochberg 2970m   Several rather dull ways up, the best being direct from the road in about 2h.   PD.

JOCHKÖPFL   3143m

122 From Timmelsjoch road.   PD.   Leave road at c2200m where the Wietenbach enters the Timmelsbach.   Follow R bank of the stream up to the Karsee, then aim for lowest pt. of ridge between Timmelsjochberg and the summit.   Follow ridge to top (3h). Alternative ways are by the SW ridge via the Rötenkarscharte (NW of Karsee), slightly more difficult, or by the less interesting short NW ridge from the col at pt.3068 (see R.124).

Ridge Traverse from Schrakogel to Siegerland hut.   Traverse is probably the wrong word, for some of the recommended route avoids the ridge altogether for snow on the N side.

123   From the Schrakogel or the col at pt.3068 cut across the glacier N of the ridge to get back on it just before summit of the Vord. Kitzkogel.   Going E from the peak, take to snow again at pt.2987 and follow E under the ridge, again rejoining crest just before next summit, Hint. Kitzkogel.   From there either reverse R.121a or R.121b down to Siegerland hut or complete the traverse by including Hohlkogel and Scheiblehnkogel as in R.120. A bit artificial but with good views.   Keeping to ridge in its entirety involves more difficult and hazardous work with very loose rock in places.

SCHRAKOGEL   3135m

124 From Timmelsjoch road.   F.   Leave road at c2200m, a little over 2 km E of the R-angle bend of the Timmelsjoch road.   Keep R of the Rotmuhrbach and (traces of path) walk quite steeply NE into the area called Rötenkarle.   Here turn E and later NE again to the small Rötenkarferner and to col at pt.3068;   then easily to the top (3h).

Wannenkogel 3088m   **Wilde Röte-Spitze** 2965m   **Rotkogel** 2892m   **Hinterer Brunnenkogel** 2775m

Undistinguished peaks in themselves.   A complete traverse of the Windachkamm peaks was described by Ludwig Purtscheller in 1892. From the Brunnenkogelhaus over the above-mentioned tops, then following ridge to the Hint. Kitzkogel with descent to the Sieger-land hut gives beautiful views of the Stubai and Ötztal Alps with no great difficulty though it takes a long time – allow some 10h. An alternative shorter and more rewarding route encompassing some of the ridge is detailed above by combining R.124, R.123.

Just toss the rope and we'll pull you out in no time.

Section 6 BOTZERKAMM

Dominated by the mountain whose name is taken for the group, this splendid snow and rock peak is best seen over the Übeltalferner from the Wilder Pfaff, Müller hut and Wilder Freiger areas. The main features are ridges extending NW and S from Botzer and its E neighbour Hochgwänd. However, apart from these 2 peaks and the ridge between Botzer and the Schwarzwandscharte to the W, there is little in the group to set pulses racing. More interest for the walker and geologist.

Hofmannspitze 3112m Small pointed rock peak immediately SE of the Schwarzwandscharte. From NW (I), 30 min. from latter col. Traverse along ridge (I) to Königshofspitze takes 30 min.

KÖNIGSHOFSPITZE 3138m E Peak 3128m W Peak

A long easy rock ridge links the 2 peaks. Snow covered to the ridge in many places on N side, steep rock on the S side and a short S ridge. Small easily traversed col at pt.3048, just E of the W peak, for access from the Übeltalferner. FA. L.Barth, L.Pfaundler, 1864 - traversed whole ridge from Schwarzwand col.

East Peak. Examples below give an opportunity to traverse the mountain with or without an additional ascent of Botzer.

125 (a) The first of 2 options from the Becherhaus. After descending the Becher rocks N to pt.3157 turn SSW following the rocky promontory and snow on its W side and passing below the hut. Then veer SW and later S to avoid crevasses and aim for the glacier bay between the E and W peaks. Get onto the ridge about 150m W of the E summit and follow it easily to top, I (2h).
(b) A second possibility from the Becherhaus takes much the same time or a little longer. From the southern foot of the Becher rocks as (a) go SSE before curving SW to snowy col just E of pt.3005. The Botzer Scharte pt.2974 is no longer an easy crossing. From this col go easily up the ridge (I).

Both these routes can be undertaken from the Müller hut, but taking a little longer, say 2h30. Leave the hut W and go down rocks steeply below the helicopter platform to glacier. After a small loop SE to avoid the icefall R, turn S to join the Becherhaus track as above. Note of caution: the Übeltalferner is a large and much crevassed glacier and can present considerable navigational problems in poor visibility. A compass and altimeter can be life-saving. In view of this the grading must be put at F+.

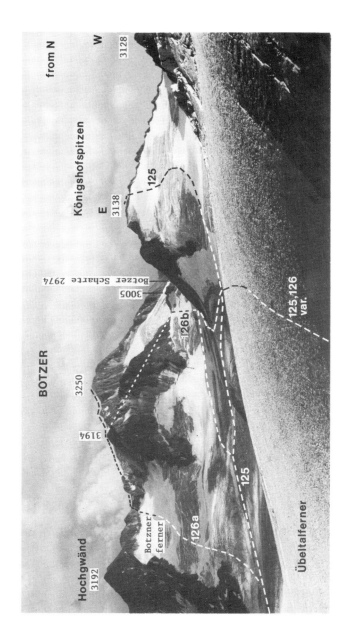

from N

W

3128

Königshofspitzen

E

3138

125

Botzer Scharte 2974

3005

BOTZER

125,126 var.

126b

3250

3194

125

Hochgwänd
3192

126a

Botzner ferner

125

Übeltalferner

An alternative southerly approach is from Timmelsalm to the
Schwarzsee, then to foot of SW ridge also called the Schneider-
lahnergrat. Some difficulty over the first rocky step then stay
on the ridge (II).
Easier, go towards the Schwarzwandscharte and up to the small
Schwarzwandferner, to the NW ridge just N of W peak (1h30 from
the Schwarzsee).

BOTZER   3250m

Principal peak of the group. All the routes are fairly straightforward (F+) given the proviso about the Übeltalferner crossing
noted above.

126   (a)   From the Becherhaus follow R.125b SSE but continue
in this line into the E bay of the Botznerferner, that is just W
of the Hochgwänd NW ridge.   Climb steeply to the short rock
ridge which separates the Botznerferner from the Hangender
Ferner and, after crossing it, turn R up slopes of the latter to
meet the Botzer N ridge as near as possible to summit (2h).
        (b)   The other way from the Becherhaus is as for R.125b;
after crossing the snowy col turn sharply E up the fairly steep
glacier slope.   Later in the season   this normally straightforward plain slope becomes very icy, crevassed and on its north-
ern aspect littered with boulders from rockfall.   Confusingly this
glacier is unnamed on the AV map but marked as Rotenferner on
some maps – on the AV map the Rötenferner is the small glacier
just S of Botzer.   At the top of the slope go R (S) up ridge or
on snow L, quickly and without difficulty to the pleasant summit (2-2h30).
As for the Königshofspitze, the Müller hut provides equally satisfactory approach routes taking slightly longer.

There is also a long and rather boring approach from Timmelsalm, winding up S of the Schwarzsee to an area called In der
Mute and reach the AV map unnamed glacier of R.126b over
scree.   This approach cannot be recommended unless you have
to come up from the S.

The SE approach from the Egetjoch and Hangender Ferner is
only worthwhile if it follows a bivouac in the Untere Senner
Egete, an attractive valley between the Egetjoch and Grohmann
hut.   Otherwise it becomes too long.

HOCHGWÄND   3192m

127 Not quite as imposing and detaining as its neighbour and
less frequently visited, even then usually in association with
Botzer. Use R.126a and get onto the fairly flat Hangender
Ferner SW of pt.3132. Turning SE, descend slightly before
climbing again, this time NE, all the while keeping not far below
the rocks of pt.3132 until reaching a pt. where a steep snow
gully leads down to the easternmost bay of the Übeltalferner

(this part of the glacier is called the Ebenerferner on ÖK 2710). From here follow W side of Hochgwänd over rocks without difficulty to the top, I (2-2h30).
The mountain can also be climbed from the E in 4h from the Grohmann hut. This is a scrappy route over steep boulders and rough scree through the Egetlahner towards pt.2805, onto the E ridge and over loose rock to the top (II).

SCHNEEBERGER WEISSEN   2968m

White rectangular block of a mountain with a jagged crest and a small glacier plus impressive screes on the N side. Best climbed from the col pt.2668 on its W side in 1h over pt.2815 with a small descent before the steepening ridge to the top.

GURTELSPITZE   2861m

Pointed rock peak which looks more inviting from a distance. The "Gurtel" or white belt at half height is obvious. Can be climbed by a roundabout route from the Gurtelscharte, between the peak and Schneeberger Weissen (see note in R.48), taking the N flank to emerge on ridge N of the top, I+. The rock is very loose (1h from col).

SCHWARZSEESPITZE   2988m

Easily reached (I) from several points including (a) Nördliche Schwarzseescharte (see R.49) and (b) from col pt.2942; dull.

MOARER WEISSEN   2967m   SPRINZENWAND   2899m

Both run S from the Schwarzseespitze, the first being easily recognised by its beautiful white colour. Both are easily climbed; Moarer Weissen by scree and a stony gully from the Schwarzsee to get onto the short N ridge, or in 1h from the Egetjoch in roundabout fashion using the small glacier remains on the mountain's N side to attain pt.2916 just N of the peak.

MOARERSPITZE   2804m

Plain mountain E of the Egetjoch, easily climbed from there in 45 min. The minor ridge extending N to the Krapfenkarspitze is straightforward but of no interest.

Section 7 SULZTALKAMM

WILDE LECK   3361m

Magnificent rock peak at S end of the Sulztalkamm – the NW
spur of the Hauptkamm. It dominates the surroundings and,
with Schrankogel, offers the most interesting climbing in the
region of the Amberger hut. The granite is superb on the E
ridge and fairly good on the other ridges though loose on the
flanks. For difficulty there is little to choose between the 3
chief ridges. Long tedious approaches from the Ötztal are not
included. Though the Amberger and Hochstubai huts are the
start-points for most of the routes, the mountain is a perfectly
feasible day-trip from the Stubaital using the Gletscherbahn to
the Eisgrat terminus and going over the Daunscharte (R.33b)
to join the Amberger hut-Wütenkarsattel track on the W side of
the Sulztalferner. If this latter approach is used, then returning via the Daunjoch and the Dresdner hut (R.33c) is easier.

East Ridge. Excellent climb on sharp solid granite. "Bier
Henkels" (the equivalent of jug-handles) abound. PD+ with 2
pitches of IV. FA of direct route: L.Pfaundler and a guide,
1895.

128   Traditionally the climb proper starts near pt.3096 where
the ridge, having been fairly level for a while, suddenly steepens. This is usually reached (a) from Hochstubai hut or Daunscharte direction by leaving the Sulztalferner at c2920m on the
Wüterkarsattel-Amberger track (R.32) at foot of a long rock
spur projecting NE from the Wütenkarspitzen. Cross these rocks
W, gaining height, thereby avoiding crevassed area of the small
Wilde Leck Ferner. Contour towards the E ridge at c3000m to
get onto the crest below pt.3096. Or (b) from the Amberger
hut leave the Wütenkarsattel track at c2860m and turn W up the
N bank of the Wilde Leck Ferner to about 3000m.

Scramble up onto ridge proper; it is best to stay on crest and
avoid only one obvious gendarme L with slight difficulty; otherwise abseil off top. The route can be made easier (III) though
less interesting by avoiding most of the tricky bits down L but
always staying as close as possible to the crest (2h30, 5h30
from Amberger, 4h from Hochstubai, about 5h30 from Eisgrat).

South Face. Originally the ordinary route, now used mainly in
descent. Technically quite an easy climb, mostly I with a few
moves II, but route finding can be tricky and the less vigilant
can stray into hostile territory. Red paint flashes at intervals
and usually enough evidence of other's passage to allay concern.
F+.

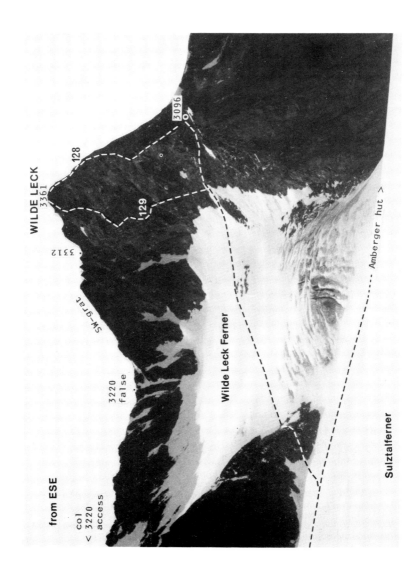

from ESE

col
< 3220
access

3220
false

SW-grat

·3312

WILDE LECK
3361

128

129

3096
o

Wilde Leck Ferner

Sulztalferner

Amberger hut >

129   Start just L of a pt. where a conspicuous scree slope runs down to the glacier from the E ridge at c3080m.   Look out for red paint and footscrapes and generally go diagonally L, back diagonally R, resume diagonally L again and finally steeper up to emerge just below and to L (SW) of the summit (1h30 from glacier, 4h30 from Amberger, 3h from Hochstubai).   In descent leave the "picnic bay" below and S of the summit cross and go SW for a few m to see the way down.

North Ridge.   Not harder than the E ridge, certainly less interesting.   Sometimes combined with a traverse of the Zahme Leck. PD+.   FA.   O.Schuster, H.Moser, 1896.

130   Leave Amberger hut to Wütenkarsattel track where a small glacier tongue runs down from between Wilde and Zahme Leck. Climb steep glacier slopes keeping N to the saddle pt.3173, so reached by easy rocks.   From here keep to the crest except to turn the broad central section R (W) (4h from Amberger hut).

South-West Ridge.   Less interest than the usual routes but has reasonable rock.   By R.128 attain the Wilde Leck Ferner and go up to col pt.3220.   Follow the ridge (I) as far as pt.3312.   From where the ridge steepens traverse L along a ledge line on the NW face (III), rteurning to the ridge a little before the summit (4h40-5h from Amberger hut).

WÜTENKARSPITZEN   3244m

Subjugated to Wilde Leck because of its relative unimportance, this is the long ridge NW of the Wütenkarsattel with 6 tops.   A complete traverse takes 2h from the Hochstubai hut to highest pt. at the NW extremity.   No special merit though an easy day from the hut or an unusual approach to the Wilde Leck SW ridge.   II.

ATTERKARSPITZEN   S Peak   3255m

3 rock peaks running NW from saddle pt.3220 at foot of the Wilde Leck SW ridge.   Isolated and rarely climbed, quite serious, III.

Zahme Leck   3226m   Sometimes traversed N-S en route for the Wilde Leck N ridge.   Can be climbed in its own right by NW and S ridges from the Amberger hut (II).

KUHSCHEIBE   3189m

131   Poor route from the Amberger hut, included because of its undoubted popularity.   Leave path to Sulztalferner at pt.2162 where a signpost indicates the direction required with the letter K.   This waymarked route leads ultimately over the Atterkarjöchl (2970m) and down to Kaisers in the Ötztal.   A small path goes SSW from just above pt.2665, up to the Rosskarferner, getting onto the summit ridge about 50m below the top, I (3h30 from hut).

Roter Kogel 3037m   **Murkarspitze** 3148m   **Muschenspitze**
3092m

Cirque of minor peaks at head of the small Murkar glacier (not
named on AV map). The Murkarspitze and Roter Kogel are quite
straightforward (I/II) from the Atterkarjöchl, a little over 3h from
the hut. The Muschenspitze has an easy short S ridge (I) and a
difficult NE ridge (also known as the Muschenschneide), III with
some exposed pitches; this climb begins at the saddle pt.2752 SW
of the Hoher Sulzkogel and takes 4-5h.

Sulzkogel Hoher 2906m   Niederer 2795m   Small rock peak
directly above and SW of the Amberger hut. Both tops can be
climbed easily (I) from the saddle between them; this is attained
tediously across grass and scree W from the Sulztal track.

REICHENKARSPITZE 2971m

The NE ridge (Schöngartachgrat) is a fairly difficult rock climb
with pitches of V; rock quite loose in places. It starts at col
pt.2767 on the SE aspect of the ridge in the Inn. Reichenkar.

This area is not easy to attain from the Sulztal, from Gries up
the good path to Nisslalm, then cross country with only traces
of path across the Äuss. Reichenkar and round the N end of the
target ridge. Descent is via S ridge to the gap pt.2890 and
down N onto the small glacier.

LOCHKOGEL 3043m   KL. LOCHKOGEL 2921m

Both have fairly difficult NE ridges with pitches of IV/V. That
of the Lochkogel involves getting onto the ridge at pt.2534 E of
the small Schönrinnenkar See (footpath from Gries). Then directly along ridge over pt.2560, 2624 and 2836 to a dramatic 8m
pinnacle. Turn this easily S and back to a small gap before the
final rise to top. The descent is S and down into the miserable
Äuss. Reichenkar. This spoils what would otherwise be quite a
good climb.

GAMSKOGEL 2815m

Mentioned because of its popularity. A simple marked path leads
S from Gries in Sulztal, going W past Nisslalm and finally winding SW to a pt. N of the summit (3h30).

Section 8 RUDERHOFSPITZE - SCHRANKOGEL
LISENSER FERNERKOGEL GROUP

From the Mutterberger Seespitze a broad rock ridge runs NE
dividing the Alpeiner valley and its lower continuation the Oberbergtal from the Falbeson valley. The group of peaks along this
ridge have glaciers of all shapes and sizes scattered among them.
A shorter and less prominent ridge extends more ENE to divide
the Falbeson valley from the Unterbergtal, down which flows the
Ruetzbach on its way from Mutterbergalm through Ranalt down to
Neustift and so on. To the W a ridge curves round the head of
the Alpeinerferner to Schrandele where a small spur extends SW
to Schrankogel then steeply down into the Sulztal. From Schrandele the main ridge runs NW to end at the Lisenser Fernerkogel with a NE spur over Wildes Hinterbergl reaching Hohe
Villerspitze. The Franz Senn hut is the best single base for
most of the peaks in this group though some of the routes are
quite long compared with others in the Stubai.

MUTTERBERGER SEESPITZE   3305m

Impressive rock mountain rising above the Bockkogelferner. The
predominantly snowy N side contrasts with the entirely rocky S
flank. No straightforward routes. The best are the NE and NW
ridges approached from Amberger hut in 4-4h30. The SW ridge
is III from the Mutterbergerjoch which is a long way from anywhere.

Bockkogel 3095m   Prominently positioned but not worthwhile because of bad rock and a laborious approach.

HÖLLTALSPITZE   3277m

132 SE Ridge/Face. Blunted pyramid, the first peak on ridge
running S from the Schwarzenbergspitzen. Long but recommended rock climb most easily approached from Dresdner hut using
the track towards the Grawagrubennieder and Neue Regensber-
ger hut (R.18) in about 90 min. IV+, some pegs in place.

Start on the ridge just W of pt. where the Hölltalscharte track
forks N from the main track. Enjoyable climbing over the much
towered lower part, then descending to a gap. Now over easy
rock to the first steep bit. Use a near vertical crack on R of
the edge to get up to a narrow horizontal fissure. Traverse 3m
R to another crack leading to an overhang. Avoid this R and
get back onto ridge. Easy rock leads to the second step. After
going over some small pinnacles either climb down a groove on

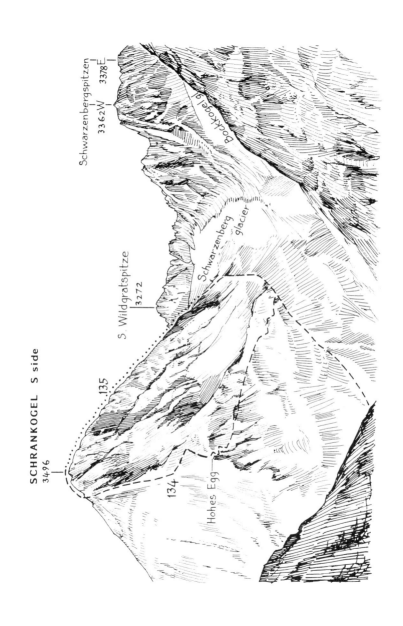

SCHRANKOGEL S side
3496

.135

S. Wildgratspitze
3272

Schwarzenbergspitzen
3362 W   3378 E

Böckkogel

Schwarzenberg glacier

134

Hohes Egg

NW side or abseil (8m). The third riser follows, exposed climbing just L of crest initially, then straddling it before it settles down to straightforward work at III on good rock up to a forepeak (large cairn). The summit lies just behind without difficulty. Descent is via the short N ridge. Go down as far as the first tower and **not** as far as the lowest pt. Climb down NE over loose rock slopes to a rock spur below which is an abseil pt. Rope down 40m over slabs and a bergschrund onto the Hölltalferner. This is much crevassed; keep above the crevasses by going NE until you can safely turn E and down to the Hölltalscharte track, which is very vague in places, R.21.

SCHWARZENBERGSPITZEN   E 3378m   W 3362m

2 impressive rock peaks connected by a sharp ridge that dominate the head of the Alpeinerferner. Rarely climbed because of comparative difficulty and proximity to the engaging and higher Ruderhofspitze and Schrankogel. The NE ridge of the E peak is the easiest way (III), about 5h from Franz Senn hut, leaving the Alpeinerferner at small col pt.3159 and climbing the first rock step directly; after a flat section turn the next steep bit L (S) and ascend slabs to the top.

WILDGRATSPITZEN   S 3272m   N 3320m

Rock peaks either side of the Wildgratscharte (see R.3) with superb close-up views of the Schrankogel NE face. The N ridge of the S peak starts fairly level and becomes increasingly steep. An enjoyable climb on good rock in about 1h30 from the Wildgratscharte (II+).
E ridge of the S peak approached from the Alpeinerferner is very loose lower down but could be used as a descent, getting onto snow of the N flank as soon as possible (I+).
S ridge of the N peak, also approached from the Wildgratscharte, takes about 1h but is a little more difficult (III).
Traverse NW to Schrandele is straightforward (I) in 45 min., but avoid the flanks; the rock is rotten.

SCHRANDELE   3393m

Rather neglected but fine rock pyramid with long ridges in all directions. The N ridge connects with Wilder Turm, the SE with the Wildgratspitzen; the SW ridge leads to Schrankogel and the E ends on W bank of the Alpeinerferner; the latter has very loose rock.

133 From South. Normal route, F. From the Wildgratscharte (R.3) descend a short slope to the Schwarzenbergferner, then follow the glacier NW to a bay at its head, c3240m. Climb broken rocks of a poorly defined gully to SE ridge above pt. 3262. Follow ridge to summit, turning some steep sections on the Schwarzenbergferner side if desired (1h from Wildgratscharte, about 5h from Franz Senn or Amberger huts).

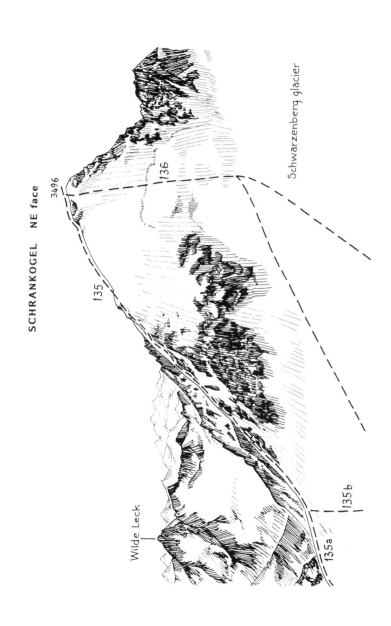

SCHRANKOGEL   NE face

3496

136

Schwarzenberg glacier

135

Wilde Leck

135b

135a

North Ridge. Rather surprisingly this was probably the route by which the mountain was first climbed though the identity of the first ascensionist(s) is disputed. A jagged ridge giving an exhilerating climb from pt.3192, a depression at the head of the Verbogenen-Berg-Ferner. The first pinnacle is turned about 30m down on R(W) side. Thereafter the crest steepens appreciably towards the summit, III (2h for ridge, 5h from Franz Senn).

SCHRANKOGEL   3496m

Second highest summit in the Stubai with a beautiful NE snow/ice face. A traverse is popular, particularly in combination with the Amberger-Franz Senn hut to hut walk. The approach from the former hut is shorter.

South-West Flank and Ridge. Once regarded as the usual way but now superceded by the E ridge. A cornice near the top can present considerable difficulties in early summer, F.

134   From Amberger hut go down to and cross the river and follow the track S then SE over grass slopes before turning E onto L bank of the Schwarzenberg stream. At c2610m the Schrankogel path breaks off L (NW). It winds up the mountainside in numerous zigzags to Hohes Egg (c2800m). Now continue NE and follow SW ridge to the summit cross: remember the possibility of awkward cornice; lot of red waymarks en route (4h).

East Ridge. Mainly rock in normal years with a short, narrow snow crest to finish. In unseasonal snow the ridge part can be arduous. More interesting than R.134, F+. One of the rare British FAs in the area: F.F.Tuckett, F.A.J.Brown with F.Biner, C.Michels, 1865.

135 (a) From Amberger hut follow R.134 to the track divergence at c2610m. Continue NE along the L side moraine until the track peters out at c3000m. Go straight up E ridge or, simpler, round its foot R to join it at a level snow section at c3100m
(b) From Franz Senn hut follow R.3 to foot of the ridge (about 4h).
Now climb the broad rock ridge with snow patches. The final section above 3400m is an elegant snow crest, short but nervy for those of anxious disposition; if at all corniced keep to the R (N) side (4h from Amberger hut, 5h from Franz Senn).

North-East Face. Beautiful snow/ice curtain seen at its best from the area of the Wildgratscharte. Highly recommended and straightforward in good conditions, 250m, AD-. The view E towards the Ötztaler Alps as you breast the ridge is worth the holiday.

136   (a) From Amberger hut reach the Schwarzenbergferner at foot of the E ridge (R.134) and head NW and later W round rocks to foot of the face.

(b) From Franz Senn hut cross the Wildgratscharte (R.3) and proceed in an arc NW, gradually turning SW and slowly gaining height reach foot of the face at c3250m (about 4h).

Climb directly to E ridge just L (E) of summit; keep just R of obvious rocks on the face just below the crest (1h).

Hinterer Wilder Turm 3294m   Vord. 3177m

Both climbed without difficulty from the Turm Scharte. The pinnacled E ridge of the Vord. gives a good rock climb in c5h from the Franz Senn hut (III/IV).

WILDES HINTERBERGL 3288m

Rounded snow dome above the Berglasferner with a steep rock flank falling W to the Schrankar.

Berglasferner route. Entirely a snow climb and a good one. The state of the glacier varies considerably but in good conditions, F.

137 From Franz Senn hut follow R.3 to the Berglas stream. Cross it and ascend grass and moraine slopes steeply to the Berglasferner snout. Continue steeply WSW up the glacier turning crevassed zones L (S) to gentler upper slopes. From c3140m, almost level with the Turm Scharte, head NW over broad snow slopes to the highest pt. at the L (W) end of the almost level and wide summit crest (4h from hut).

Verborgenen Berg Ferner route. Easier than R.137 and thoroughly recommended to all. It avoids significantly crevassed areas, F.

138 From Franz Senn hut take R.3 up R side of the Alpeinerferner to a little over 2700m where a small track leads WNW over scree and snow patches under E ridge of the Vord. Turm to the Turm Scharte, pt.3154. Then easily NW over gentle snow slopes to summit (about 4h from hut).

North-West Ridge. From the Brunnenkogelscharte in 30 min. (II), staying on ridge though avoiding a small tower on the Schrankar side. This can be combined with the Hint. Brunnenkogel (R.139) and makes a pleasant round day trip from the Franz Senn hut, descending via R.137 or R.138.

An alternative steep snow/ice slope from the Lisenserferner, about 80m high, emerges more or less at the highest pt., PD+.

HINTERER BRUNNENKOGEL   3325m

Attractive rock pyramid above the Lisenserferner with a steep
W face. Fairly easy from Franz Senn, Amberger and Westfalen
huts.

South-East Ridge. An enjoyable climb from the Brunnenkogelscharte, PD-. Avoiding 2 pinnacles at the start makes it easier
but unsatisfying. FA. L.Seibert, G.Kichler, M.Egger, T.Siller,
1889.

139 From Franz Senn hut take R.141 to the Innere Rinnennieder (2h). On W side of the col descend slightly onto the
Lisenserferner and head SW up its gentle slopes to the Brunnenkogelscharte (3212m), guarded by a bergschrund at foot of
the SE ridge (1h30). (The Berglas-Übergang is a shorter but
much more difficult way to the same pt., PD/AD depending on
condition of the hanging glacier at head of the Berglastal, itself reached directly W up and out of the Alpeiner valley after
following R.3 as far as the Berglas stream).
From the Scharte a good slab pitch starts the climb. The first
pinnacle is traversed and a second turned on the Schrankar
side. During this latter manoeuvre note a steep corner with
some exposure though good holds (III); it leads from an apparently inescapable position back to the ridge and quickly to pt.
3273, a gap with a short snow crest. The final section is easy
though steep scrambling on good rock. Stay on the crest here;
the flanks are quite loose (1-1h30, 4h40-5h from hut).

140 South-West Ridge. Less frequented, scrappy but no difficulties, F. FA. L.Purtscheller, F.Schnaiter, 1880.

   (a) From the Westfalenhaus follow R.4 (Dr Siemons Weg) to
the Längentaljoch (2991m) (3h).
   (b) From Amberger hut reverse R.4 up through the Schrankar to the Längentaljoch (3h).
Now climb lower section of ridge; about 100m above the pass
traverse R onto the SW flank and scramble up steep broken rock
(I) to summit (1h, about 4h from either hut).

North-East Ridge. Jagged crest of sound rock (III/IV) climbed
from the Brunnenkogelnieder (pt.3124) reached by gentle snow
slopes from the E, or from W side by the third Brunnenkogelrinne (see below).

Brunnenkogelrinnen These 3 large gullies are cut into the
steep W flank of the Brunnenkogel ridge. All 3 offer transit
between the Längental and the Lisenserferner. The southernmost, designated the third, is the easiest (I+). The 3 are
marked on AV 31/2; 31/1 includes only the 3rd, southernmost
crossing and this is indicated only by pt.3124. None are
recommended because of loose rock and stonefall. See also
note after R.60.

VORDERER BRUNNENKOGEL   3306m

A rock peak with no easy way up. The S and NE ridges are III
and a traverse gives a good climb in about 8h door to door from
the Franz Senn hut. The NW face is considered one of the finest
rock climbs in the Stubai, serious, surmounting a 470m wall with
one pitch of V+. It also has the doubtful reputation of unpredictable rock. It starts just S of the 2nd Brunnenkogelrinne.

Lisenserspitze 3230m   Rotgratspitze 3273m

2 minor summits of easy access, the former from S or E in 30 min.
from the Lisenserferner, the latter in about 15 min. from the col
between the peak and Lisenser Fernerkogel. The S face of the
Rotgratspitze has a selection of good rock climbs, 200m, III to V.

LISENSER FERNERKOGEL   3299m

Majestic rock peak towering 1600m above the head of the Lisens
valley. The panorama from its summit is considered one of the
finest in the Eastern Alps. FA. P.C.Thurwieser, P.Schöpf, 1836.

Ordinary Route. The only popular way up, full of scenic variety, strongly recommended and straightforward. It looks particularly impressive and quite daunting from the Innere Rinnennieder but is easier than it looks, F. FA. H.Buchner and
F.Jenewein, 1876.

141   From Franz Senn hut take the Horntaler Joch path N as
far as c2200m where it divides. Follow the Rinnensee/spitze
track, climbing SW into the Rinnen cirque, eventually arriving
at N edge of the Rinnensee (2650m), 1h10min. The view S from
here of the Seespitzen particularly is superb, a well known
picture postcard; snow-capped peaks reflected in the waters of
the small lake. The path then winds up gradually N, reaching
the Innere Rinnennieder (2902m) via a miserable shaly gully
(red waymarks, 50 min.). Lovely view of the target from here.
Go down a short snow slope to the glacier (sometimes a small
bergschrund) and cross it WNW (crevasses) to foot of the rock
barrier, Plattige Wand. The glacier crossing is long, about
1.5 km, and route finding can be difficult in poor visibility.
This is particularly true in the reverse direction as the Inn.
Rinnennieder may be tricky to locate. The Plattige Wand looks
insurmountable from a distance but you slant up broken rocks
diagonally L to R; a few cairns, vague traces. So reach the
Rotgratferner at pt.3045. Now more steeply up this slope,
first NW then W, to the saddle pt.3198 between Lisenser Fernerkogel and the Rotgratspitze. Finally scramble up the S ridge
easily (about 4h from hut).

North (glacier) route. Alternative approach to the upper Lisenserferner, infrequently used. The path is not always easy
to follow and the glacier is rarely tracked.

ROTGRATSPITZE   LISENSER FERNERKOGEL

3299

141

3198

3273

141

Plattige Wand

Lisenserferner

from SE

142 From Lisens take path on E side of the Melach stream to the Fernerboden. Where the Winterweg to the Westfalenhaus (R.58) goes R continue until at c1800m the small path winds E up a steep meadow to a ruined hut, then slants L(NE) to a rock barrier and above doubles back R over steep grass slopes and broken rocks to the beginning of the Kl. Horntal. Cross a tiny stream R and go SSE along the moraine ridge to pt.2433. Polished rocks now lead to the Lisener glacier. Ascend its R bank (crevasses) until W of the Äuss. Rinnennieder, then head SW to join R.141 at c2880m W of the Inn. Rinnennieder (about 5h30 to top).

North Ridge. Long, some loose rock, but generally regarded as a good climb. FA. L.Purtscheller, E.Rofner (in descent), 1877.

143 Use the winter path from Lisens towards the Westfalenhaus (R.58); some 200m before the Längentaler Alm climb S up steep grass slopes. First traverse L to R up through the lower rock girdle at the easiest pt., then climb about 40m higher on stone and grass covered flanks to foot of the ridge proper. Now get onto the duplicated ridges initially on the eastern and higher up on the westernmost to the N forepeak; then stay on the now single ridge less steeply to the top (3h30 from the Alm). PD+.

BERGLASSPITZE 3125m

Imposing summit with all routes requiring some competence. The simplest is the SE ridge; leave R.141 above the Rinnensee and go up the southern slopes of the Rinnen glacier (unnamed on AV map) to pt.2934, a small col where you join the ridge. Turn some harder bits L (S), exposed in places, II (3h from hut).

The NE ridge, reached from a steep scree gully a little way SW of the Inn. Rinnennieder, is II. The SW ridge is rather longer (II) and reached by rounding the mountain N on the Lisenserferner to a pt. just N of the Berglas-Übergang. Take W flank until the ridge steepens then stay on the crest until it bends. Here there is a 2m gap; follow ensuing ridge to the top.

RINNENSPITZE 3003m

Rock peak between Inn. and Äuss. Rinnennieder above the Rinnensee with fine views. The E flank is the normal way up, following R.141 from the Franz Senn hut until a little above 2600m where an obvious track bears R and ascends over steepish grass and scree, so followed easily to the peak; dull, F.

144 South-West Ridge. A good route from the Inn. Rinnennieder (R.141), PD+. FA. J.Pock, Alliani, 1892. From the col climb directly NE to a tower. Follow the crest down and turn 2 gendarmes L. Many parties start the ascent here usually from the Lisenserferner. Now up the ridge again to a gap, after

which is a large overhang. Turn this L where there is a short
groove (crux). Use this to return to the ridge, III (about
1h30 from the Rinnennieder, 3h30 from the Franz Senn).

Kreuzkamp 3008m   **Blechnerkamp** 3000m   Rarely visited.
Can be traversed from the Kl. Horntalerjoch to the Äuss. Rinnennieder without difficulty, never more than II. From Äuss.
Rinnennieder descend SE to the Rinnensee - Franz Senn hut
path. About 5h for the round trip.

Schafgrübler 2921m   Frequently climbed on account of its simp-
licity and the view; 20 min. from the Horntalerjoch (R.145).   The
traverse to the Kl. Horntalerjoch over the insignificant Horntaler-
spitze is also easy.

HOHE VILLERSPITZE   3092m

Seen from the S as an imposing rock peak and sited at pt. where
the ridge divides to enclose the Fotschertal and its small glacier
(Fotscherferner) to the N. All the routes are rock climbs.   FA.
K.Gsaller (solo), 1878.

From Horntalerjoch. Quite a nice short climb, PD-.

145   From Franz Senn hut follow R.46 to pt. where the Wildkop-
fscharte/Potsdamer hut/Seejöchl etc. path forks R. Go L here
(signpost Horntalerjoch) and climb more steeply over a rocky
shoulder into a grassy basin, then over another shoulder with the
Horntalerjoch coming into view.   The path crosses snow patches
and ultimately climbs steeply towards the pass (2h).   Note that
the pass can also be reached from Lisens on a steep marked path
in 3h or so.
Where the path turns W towards the pass go R up steep grass
well N of the Joch to start on S ridge of the mountain close to
pt. where it steepens considerably.   The ridge subsequently mer-
ges with the SE and W faces of the mountain.   Initially follow E
side of ridge along an obvious path near the crest and soon
crossing over to the W side.   A R turn up a slabby slope soon
regains the crest.   Continue over small pinnacles or just below
on the E side to reach a gap above a gully where there is a
small cairn.   Now make a rising traverse on W face along a small
path followed by a steeper rock step above considerable exposure.   This section is called Schiefe Gang (sloping gangway).   At
an obvious scree platform turn R into a deeply cut rock gully,
stonefall danger, one pitch II+, pegs here and there.   Higher up
take the L fork to a crest with a small subsidiary summit just L.
Turn R (E) and follow ridge to top; it steepens as you cross the
head of the R branch of the gully (1h30 for ridge, 3h30 from
hut).

It is also perfectly feasible as a day trip from Oberiss Alm up through the Viller Grube. A small path is shown on AV map going NW then W to intersect with R.46 to help you on the way.

North-West Ridge. Over the Lisenser Villerspitze, a pleasant roundabout way, PD. The latter lies on ridge running NW then N from the Hohe Villerspitze on W side of the Fotschertal. FA. O.Melzer, M.Peer, 1894.

146 Follow R.147 to Lisenser Villerspitze (4h). Go down broken rocks S to pt.2932 and continue on the straightforward crest to 2 knolls which are traversed (II). Then keep to the sharp crest as much as possible (II), turning a few steep bits L on the N face (beware loose rock) to summit (2h, 6h from Potsdamer hut).

The E ridge (also called Schaldersgrat) offers a long route from the Schaldersjöchl, itself reached from the Franz Senn or Potsdamer huts. It crosses the Schaldersspitze and Grawa Wand, III in places, 6-7h from the huts. This can be abbreviated by starting the ridge above a scree gully running up from the Viller Grube.

LISENSER VILLERSPITZE 3026m

More an extension of the Hohe Villerspitze than a peak in its own right. Usually climbed in association with the latter, F+.

147 From Potsdamer hut take the signposted path more or less level and running SW. Fork R (signpost) at a track crossing about one km from the hut. At the Inn. Bremstall the path bears W to reach the Hochgrafljoch (2695m) over scree and often snow, steepening nearer the pass (2h30). From Lisens a path leads over the foot of the Lisenser Villerspitze NW ridge and up the Schönlisenstal to the pass in 3h.
Now descend 30m on the W side of the pass until a narrow valley opens on the L (SW). Go up its boulder slopes to join the mountain's NE ridge beyond pt.2822. It narrows to a lower top pt.2981. On the other side drop a few m and climb the slabby crest (II) to top (1h30, 4h from hut).
Minor peaks N and NE of Hohe Villerspitze are less interesting.

Hohe Rote 2828m   Just N of the Hochgrafljoch, best climbed from Schönlisens Alm over grass and boulders; dull.

Roter Kogel 2834m   Only really frequented as a ski touring peak. Marked path in summer from the Potsdamer hut and from Praxmar; not very diverting.

RUDERHOFSPITZE 3473m

Third highest peak in the Stubai, popular outing particularly from the Franz Senn hut though also done from the Neue Regensburger. The NW ridge and N face offer excellent climbs.

FA. K.Bädecker, A von Ruthner, P.Gleinser, A.Tanzer, by normal route, 1864.

Ordinary West Route. Mostly over glacier (often well tracked) with a scramble to finish, F/F+.

148 (a) From Franz Senn hut follow R.3 to c3000m on the Alpeinerferner to a pt. due E of the Wildgratscharte. Continue S then SE, gaining height gradually until approx. due N of the Hölltalscharte at c3120m. Now go E passing some large crevasses into the glacier basin below the summit. In recent years the usual route has changed here and does not follow that suggested by the AV map. Gullies coming down from the SW ridge are now often subject to stonefall and the bergschrund crossing may be difficult. Most parties now use the Obere Hölltalscharte (3247m), then follow ridge, over easy broken rocks and snow, on or just to R of ridge to the summit cross which is approached for the last few m from the E (5h30 from hut).

(b) From Neue Regensburger hut follow R.18 to the Falbesonersee. Ascend the R (N) bank moraine N of pt.2755, a rock outcrop, to get onto the glacier at c2800m; go up the R (N) side below steep rock flank of the Östl. Seespitze, before heading SW to the Hochmoosscharte, 3231m (2h30-3h). On the W side descend a steep scree/snow slope to the Alpeiner glacier and go down it WSW to c3040m before contouring roughly SW to join the Franz Senn route at c3080m E of the Schwarzenbergjoch. Trying to cut the corner off this circuitous route can lead to difficulties in a crevassed zone W of the W spur of the mountain; long and not recommended (hut to summit, 6h).

(c) From Dresdner hut follow R.21 to the Hölltalscharte. Go up ridge towards the Obere Hölltalscharte pt.3247. The rocky knoll pt.3260 can either be traversed (awkward) or turned R(S) easily. Then take ridge directly almost to the summit with no particular difficulties, as (a) (6h).

Grawawand glacier route. A good snow climb from the Regensburger hut and much more interesting than going over the Hochmoosscharte, F. FA. J.Scholz and companions, 1883.

149 Take R.18 to the Grawagrubennieder. Now keep below the Grawawand wall on N side of the Grawawandferner. At c3200m climb the steep fairly narrow snow/ice couloir on the R or L of the rocky promontory which divides it, then going NW towards pt.3435 though keeping it to your R. Continue up snow slopes to ridge just E of summit and follow it to the cross (4h).

North-West Ridge. Entertaining scramble from the Hochmoosscharte, PD. FA. K. & R.Kerschbaum, J.Pfurtscheller, 1895.

150 From Regensburger hut take R.148b to the Hochmoosscharte; or from the Franz Senn start by R.148a and reverse appropriate part of R.148b to col. From here climb to pt.3395 (II), avoiding a harder pitch L(E) of the crest at the first steep bit, but stay on the better rock of the crest wherever possible. A short descent leads to a level scree section. Confronted by a prominent rock step, either climb it directly (hard) or turn it one rope length down the gully R with an obvious exit L. Then go up the flank back to ridge. Now easy sound rock leads to top (5h from Neue Regensburger, rather more from the Franz Senn).

North Face.   A fine ice wall rising from the Hochmoosferner. Slightly harder than the Schrankogel NE face, 200m, AD. Can reach 60° at the ice bulge but the whole exercise becomes much simpler the further L you go to start; this is improper. FA. A.Pensch, E.Renk, 1926.

151   From Regensburger hut follow R.18 and R.148b to just below the Hochmoosscharte. At c3200m head SSW to foot of the face (3h30). Start L of summit fall line and climb straight up to the obvious ice bulge which can be rounded L or R and slant back to snow which runs almost to the summit cross (1h, 4h30 from hut). It is fashionable with local guides to do a short and easier variation still steep enough to be interesting. Cross the glacier SSW as above but go to the bottom of the face close to the rocks of the NE ridge. Cross the bergschrund and climb SW to the snow col E of the summit.

SEESPITZEN   ÖSTL. 3416m   WESTL. 3355m

Sometimes known as the Falbesoner Seespitzen after the small lake below the Hochmoosferner. Important summits diminished by popularity of the adjacent Ruderhofspitze. Frequently traversed, this sometimes as part of a transfer from Franz Senn to Neue Regensburger huts, but the E peak is most commonly done as a day trip from the Franz Senn.   FA. L.Barth, L.Pfaundler, 1863 (SE ridge).

152 Alpeiner Kräulferner normal route.   F.   From Franz Senn hut go along the track SW towards the Alpeinerferner. After the knoll W of pt.2204 a rough track ascends L side of the valley and moves up the moraine to the Alpeiner Kräulferner; this is usually easier than trying to cross the glacier higher up. Keep L of the crevassed zone and climb SE towards pt.3259, the lowest pt. between the Südl. Kräulspitze and Östl. Seespitze. Just below this veer R to the snowy E ridge and so quickly to the top (5h).
The traverse to the Westl. Seespitze is a straightforward mixed ridge. Descend SW to pt.3305 and go up the short E ridge to top of the Westl. From here the descent of the rock ridge and snow slope to the Hochmoosscharte is easy (8h for the whole expedition and back to hut).

RUDERHOFSPITZE W side

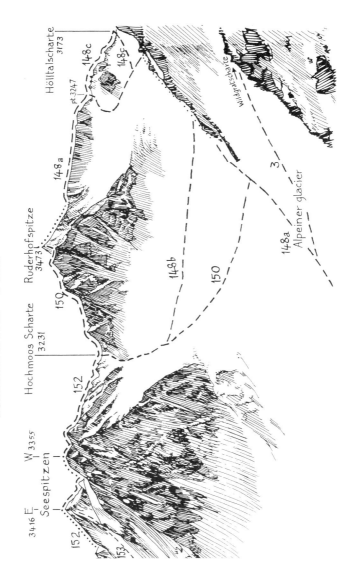

Hölltalscharte 3173
148c
148c
pt. 3247
148a
Ruderhofspitze 3473
Hochmoos Scharte 3231
W 3355
3416 E
Seespitzen
152
152
152
152
150
150
150
148b
148a
Alpiner glacier
3
Wildgratscharte

153 Seespitzferner route. Excellent ice climb with an interest-ing finish, AD. From Franz Senn hut follow R.3 to c2280m just after crossing the Berglas stream where a small path goes up R bank of Alpeiner stream. Further up on glacier proper move acr-oss SE to where a narrow snow runnel falls from the Seespitzfern-er to glacier floor. Climb this (odd rocks) to a small snow plat-eau at c2900m. Take the glacier snout direct, harder on the R with a maximum gradient of c50°, to where the slope eases. Con-tinue directly towards the peak over gentler slopes and soon cross a bergschrund, usually straightforward. A snow gully runs almost directly down from the summit; climb it - some care needed with loose rock (5h). An alternative to this steep gully is to move R and find the easiest line to the ridge.

153a Another possible ice climb on this mountain follows R.152 up the Alpeiner Kräulferner to where the gradient eases at c2900m, there crossing to S side of the glacier and climbing with increas-ing steepness E, still on the glacier and gradually turning S tow-ards the summit.

154 South-East Ridge. From Regensburger hut take R.18 and R.148b onto the Hochmoosferner and go up R side as for the Hochmoosscharte to c3150m. Climb NE over snow then rocks to the peak without difficulty. An alternative is to take the ridge more or less entirely, starting from the Hochmoosferner and climbing N onto the ridge (II). Neither version has a lot to recommend it.

KRÄULSPITZEN

The 3 tops form almost a semi-circle, enclosing to their SE the Falbesoner Kräulferner. The ridge running W from the N peak makes a R-angled turn at the middle peak and continues S to the S peak. Steep snow slopes cover the N flank of the middle peak above the Sommerwandferner; an unpleasant loose rockface drops SE to the Falbesoner Kräulferner. The Sommerwandferner side of the N peak is steep rock whilst on the NE side the Fal-besoner Knotenferner rises almost to the top. The traverse described below is merely one of a number.

Südliche Kräulspitze   3289m

Least significant of the 3, most easily climbed by its short S ridge from a depression pt.3259, F. R.152 (for the Östl. See-spitze) leads to latter pt. which can also be reached over the Falbesoner Kräulferner from the Regensburger hut. FA. H.Kober, M.Vogelmayer, F.Permoser, 1889.

Mittlere Kräulspitze   3302m

FA. L.Purtscheller, 1890 - direct from NE side snow and rocks.

The direct approach is as for the traverse, R.156, over the Sommerwandferner and the Kräulscharte (pt.3069), though it is possible to avoid the rocky hump pt.3142 by using the snow bay NW of the summit. Subsequently stay on ridge to the top, II, about 4h from the Franz Senn. It can also be climbed from the SE off the Falbesoner Kräulferner to the small col pt.3228 S of the peak, with only a short steep bit to follow; loose rock, II (about 4h from Regensburger hut).

Nördliche Kräulspitze   3292m

155   FA. L.Purtscheller, 1890 (E ridge). Climbed as in the traverse (R.156) or from Regensburger hut via the Falbesoner Knotenferner, F. The ascent to the glacier to start the ascent is a bit tiresome. From Regensburger hut follow R.18 to the stream coming down from the Falbesoner Knotenferner. Ascend scree and broken rock L (W) of stream in a NW direction to the moraine ridge. Go W up the glacier towards a rock tongue which projects N from the Hint. Plattenspitze - Nördl. Kräulspitze connecting ridge. At c2960m slant SW to foot of the Hint. Plattenspitze (ie. turning the rock tongue L) and continue up on the R (N) side of the connecting ridge to summit (3h30).

Kräulspitzen Traverse. Ridges entirely of rock; glaciers to begin and finish if starting from Franz Senn hut. Described N to S but equally good in the opposite direction, PD. It can be extended by starting on one of the Knotenspitzen with the additional advantage of thus excluding the otherwise inevitable ascent followed by descent of the Nördl. Kräulspitze W ridge.

156   From Franz Senn hut follow the Vord. Sommerwand path S into the area called Stiergschwez. After turning SW the path peters out as indicated on AV map just after a small lake. It is better to ascend the W aspect of the Sommerwandferner, keeping R of the obvious rock island to avoid a heavily crevassed area. Then aim directly towards the Kräulscharte but turn SE from c2950m. Climb a steep snow slope (bergschrund) and broken rocks to saddle c3240m between Nördl. and Mittl. Kräulspitzen and go along W ridge to the N peak (this short cut has become more difficult in recent years and the easier though longer option is to traverse the lot from the Kräulscharte). Keep to the spiky ridge and turn an obvious steep step R (S) on good rock (3h30 from hut). Reverse this part to the saddle again and climb the middle peak by its E ridge, II (1-1h30). From this summit descend a rock gully SW on R side of the S ridge then follow the crest. Turn a big step R (W) till slightly lower than pt.3228, a saddle on the ridge, and cross to it. Traverse the next pinnacle to another gap and continue along ridge over a hump to the S peak, II (1h, 5h30-6h from hut).
Go down the short S ridge to pt.3259, a minor depression, NW onto the upper slopes of the Alpeiner Kräulferner and reverse R.152.
Note: You can also start from the Regensburger hut by R.155.

ÖSTLICHE KNOTENSPITZE   3100m

Rugged rock cone with a minor peak, the Kreuzspitze, 10 min.
to the S where the ridge bends WSW. Traversing the mountain
offers a much more interesting route from the Franz Senn to
Regensburger huts than the usual crossings of the Schrimmennieder or the Hochmoosscharte.

157 South Flank. A path as far as the Kreuzspitze, then a
short scramble, F. The small now easier to find signposted
track starts immediately outside the Regensburger hut and leads
NW towards the Jedlasgrüblferner. At c2780m, E of the Vord.
Plattenspitze, the track bends N, snow patches here in early
summer. For a while little height is gained, then scramble
steeply up the S flank to the Kreuzspitze. Now descend slightly into a gap, beyond keeping L below crest for a few m to
a cairn, before bearing R back up to the ridge which soon leads
to the trig. marker on top (I/I+ for ridge direct, 10 min. peak
to peak, 2h from hut).

North Ridge (Gschwezgrat). From the summit a long ridge
falls NW to pt.2852 then N to the Oberisserscharte, thereafter rising slightly over some minor humps before dropping
to the Oberberg valley. This latter lower section is avoided.
Fairly easy with pleasant situations, II.

158 From Franz Senn hut cross the stream and head SE
across grass and boulders to the Oberisserscharte (1h).
Follow ridge without difficulty; higher up boulder slopes
on L reach the crest. Later it is easier to go onto a snow
tongue L(E) of ridge and climb it to the saddle SE of
pt.2852. Then the ridge steepens. Turn the first section
R(W). When the ridge becomes less well defined traverse
L to a chimney on N side above a long slabby gully. Climb
it (II) back to crest and cross a broad scree terrace R on
the W flank, up to SW ridge just below the summit (2-2h30,
3-3h30 from hut).

Falbesoner Knotenspitze   3120m   Of little interest in its own
right and really only worthwhile as part of a traverse of the
Knotenspitzen. Can be climbed from Franz Senn hut by its N
ridge (I) or by ascending the central branch of the Knotensp-
itzferner and up broken rocks to the saddle pt.3068 before taking ridge to summit, F (3h).

Alpeiner Knotenspitze   3233m   Fine triangular rock peak dominating the Sommerwandferner but lacking any good climbs. As
a one-off, can be climbed easily from pt.3068 as mentioned above.
The NNE spur has very loose rock and is not recommended.

159 Knotenspitzen Traverse. From the Östl. Knotenspitze the
traverse to the Falbesoner Knotenspitze involves some exposed

pitches of II/II+ beyond the lowest pt. Loose rock abounds. In any case much of the ridge can be turned R on the Knotenspitzenferner (1h30). From there on to the Alpeiner Knotenspitze is straightforward. There are 2 short sharp breaks in the ridge which can be turned L (S) without difficulty, then follow a shattered ridge to top (1h). Continuation to the Nördl. Kräulspitze presents no problems and beyond gap at pt.3196 the ridge can be avoided at will along upper edge of the Falbesoner Knotenferner (1h30).

It will be appreciated from the above notes that there are endless permutations and possibilities embracing the Kräulspitsen, the Knotenspitzen and the Seespitzen either as traverse tours in themselves or as part of a transfer between Franz Senn and Regensburger huts.

Sommerwände   Inn. 3122m   Hint. 2904m   Mitt. 2847m   Vord. 2677m   These 4 summits run generally SSW from the Franz Senn hut towards the Kräulscharte. On AV 31/1 the Mittl. peak is wrongly attributed to pt.2801. It actually lies further SW at pt.2847. The whole lot can be traversed with only an occasional pitch of III, some exposed climbing and reasonable rock. There is a small path from the Franz Senn to the Vord. top which leaves R.156 at c2600m after 1h. This is a good viewpoint and a straightforward walk (1h30). Start the traverse here. One can escape easily on the Sommerwandferner side either end of the Mitt. peak. Finish at the Kräulscharte and allow 6-7h for the trip. Alternatively the Inn. Sommerwand is a pleasant climb in its own right via the Kräulscharte, II (3h30).

Uelasgratspitze   Just NE of the Östl. Knotenspitze, taking its name from its N ridge (Uelasgrat), giving a rock climb of III+ from the Franz Senn hut (4h). The jagged ridge SW to the Östl. Knotenspitze has pitches of IV (3h). Other routes, including the E ridge climbed from the Regensburger hut (II, 3h), are uninteresting.
    Minor peaks NE of the Schrimmennieder are generally of no interest to the climber.

Brennerspitze   2882m   Situated in the angle between the Stubaital and the Oberbergtal. Mentioned only because it can look impressive and encouraging, especially if snow covered, from Neustift. The E ridge is easily attained from Milderaunalm but those seeking a training walk should beware. It is not only tiresome walking but also almost 2000m from valley to summit.

Grawawand   3338m   3167m   Long serrated ridge running E from the Ruderhofspitze and falling abruptly to the Grawagrubennieder. Very loose in places.

Nockwand 3091m   Much plagued by stonefall but a fairly secure route is the W ridge, approached from the Grawagruben-nieder (II). Stay on ridge though avoiding the prominent gend-arme R (S) (1-1h30).

Pfandlspitze 3025m   The easiest route is from the S up grass and rock slopes to saddle pt.2948 between the peak and the Nock-wand, then take the SW ridge to top. The N side routes are hard and not especially recommendable.

The altimeter's working well now.

Section 9 NORTH-WEST STUBAI

Generally a much less frequented area with a number of good rock and mixed routes though the glaciers are smaller than elsewhere. The mountains allocated to this empirical topograph-ical grouping lies within the quadrilateral described by the Sell-raintal to the N, the Ötztal to the W and the Sulztal to the S. The E border is arbitrarily formed by a line from the Sulztal across the Längentaljoch to the Westfalenhaus, extending into the Lisensertal and thus back to the Sellraintal.

The main ridges are as follows. From the Acherkogel SSE to the Hochreichkopf and Hohe Wasserfalle, E to the Kraspesspitze where the ridge makes a R-angled turn to continue S over the Sonnenwände to the Winnebacher Weisskogel. From here a west-erly branch extends via the Larstigspitze and Strahlkogel to the Grasstaller Griesskogel. Further S Hoher Seeblaskogel and the Bachfallen group of peaks enclose the glacier of the same name.

MANINGKOGEL   2892m

Easily identified and nicely shaped small rock peak at end of the Acherkogel NE ridge. Easily climbed (I) from col pt.2850.

160   North-East Ridge. One of the best middle grade rock routes in the area, perhaps in the Stubai. Often combined with Acher-kogel NE ridge, R.162. AD-. Use R.10 towards the Mittertal-scharte and make a beeline for bottom of the ridge, passing small lake on the way. Initially it is easier to climb on N side of the ridge. Difficulties begin some 150m up where the ridge narrows. The first riser is taken direct (IV). Subsequently keep mainly on the crest, occasionally using slabs on the S side, to the top. More difficult if keeping to the ridge throughout but generally III; allow 2h30 for ridge.

A recommended hard route on the N face, the Luftballonweg, was first climbed in 1986 (H.Gogl, P.Ohnmacht). The wall is 350m high, 11 pitches, starting 250m R of the NE ridge start. One pitch VI with an aid point and a few VI-.

ACHERKOGEL   3008m

Splendid rock pyramid above Oetz with sharp ridges and steep flanks. FA. L.Purtscheller, J.Schnaiter, 1881 (by a route from the SE no longer used). The original SW flank normal route first climbed in 1891 is rarely done, being hard to follow and objectively dangerous from stonefall. The mountain is only occ-asionally climbed from the Dortmunder hut in Kühtai, taking the marked path towards the Mittertalscharte, heading through the Rossböden to the tiny Mittertalferner, then up towards a small col on S ridge of the Acherkogel, PD, about 5h.

161 North Flank Route. Now the accepted normal route, F+.
FA. O.Melzer, 1893. From Bielefelder hut reverse R.11 to site
of the old hut destroyed by avalanche in 1951 (45-60 min.).
(Note that the Wetterkreuz track branches NE in steep zigzags
before this at c2200m). Now turn L (E) up towards the Mittertalscharte (see also R.10). At c2500m move S to the small Man-
ingsee (30 min.). Go round its R side (traces of path, cairns)
through a short gully and across and up a snowfield (broken
rocks later in the season) to bottom of a slabby step with a
stream R. Ascend this to the upper snowfield. Now go up the
obvious rock rib on R of the snow, up the N face of the mountain, aiming for a pt. just L (E) of obvious cross on W subsidiary
summit. There are some red waymarks. On reaching the summit ridge turn L (E) and traverse a small knoll to the true top,
in 1988 a broken wooden cross and a Gipfelbuch (3h30).

North-East Ridge. A good climb from the col pt.2850 between the
Maningkogel and Acherkogel, AD-. FA. K.Holzhammer, 1924.

162 As for R.161 to snowfield on the N flank, then up towards
the col pt.2850. Getting onto the ridge directly is not easy, cIV.
Then stay on the exposed crest over a short knife edge stretch
on sound rock with good holds. A few pitches of III+ mostly in
the upper half. A few difficult bits can be turned on the R (4h
from hut).
Traverse to the Grosser Wechnerkogel is quite hard (IV) and
takes at least 3h.

GROSSER WECHNERKOGEL 2955m

Fine pointed rock peak when seen from the Acherkar, taking its
name from Carl Wechner, an early Innsbruck climber. Much less
frequented than the Acherkogel and Maningkogel.

South Ridge. The most straightforward way, a bit tedious in the
middle reaches and probably better used as a descent for R.164.
Nevertheless a nice top and the peaceful Längental make it worthy
of inclusion, F.

163 Leave Kühtai near the Dortmunder hut on the track signed
for the Niederreichscharte up the Längental. It soon becomes a
relatively little used path with blue waymarks which, confusingly,
suddenly change to red above the small lake pt.2088. Follow the
pleasant stream on its E and S banks, turning sharply W at c2300m.
Here the way is more accurately shown on ÖK 2705 and the AV map
is incorrect. Certainly the path hereabouts becomes vague but
crosses the stream to its N bank at c2350m, turning sharply NW
away from the stream up towards some small pools where it becomes easier to follow and is similar to that marked on the AV map.
Now up towards the Niederreichscharte, steepening suddenly at
c2500m and soon taking a sharp L (S) turn. At this pt. head
rather N of W into boulders and snow patches, aiming for a pt.
on the Gr. Wechnerkogel S ridge just N of the Längentaler Turm.

It can be reached almost anywhere but easiest is via an obvious series of ledges like ramps. The ridge is of sound rock, II in places, though any transient difficulties can be turned on the looser E flank reducing it to a scramble (3h).

164 East Ridge. An excellent climb from the Wechnerscharte, II. Approach as for the Acherkogel E flank from the Dortmunder hut (Kühtai) until reaching the Mittertalferner. Go up SE over the fairly steep glacier under the Wechnerwand and up to the Wechnerscharte. A small tower divides this into E and W gaps. Take the easier to reach the E-most of these and turn the tower on its S side. This pt. can also be reached over loose and unpleasant ground from the Längental. The first bit is quite loose but the rock soon improves. Once on the ridge the steeper pitches can be turned L then R but it is better done more or less direct. Finally after a gap the ridge rises over slabs, avoidable L if preferred, to the top (5h).

HOCHREICHKOPF   3008m

Cone shaped mountain between the Niederreich and Hochreich Schartes; can be approached from the Bielefelder, Dortmunder and Gubener huts.

165 South Flank. The easiest way, F. FA. L.Purtscheller, 1890. From Gubener hut follow R.11 to the Hochreichscharte (3h), then over scree and broken rocks in 20 min. to top (3h30 from hut).

166 North-West Ridge. Somewhat loose, F. (a) From Dortmunder hut follow R.163 up the Längental. After the sharp SW turn above 2500m the path continues over tiresome boulders and scree slopes, sometimes snow covered, to the Niederreichscharte (2728m) (3-3h30). Or (b), from Bielefelder hut reverse R.11 to the Niederreichscharte (3h30-4h).
From the col a small track zigzags up the NW ridge. At c2890m there is a path down R for the Hochreichscharte which bypasses the summit across W flank of the mountain. At this pt. continue steeply on ridge (II) until the crest levels out towards the top (1h).

Hohe Wasserfalle 3002m   On the ridge S of the Hochreichscharte (see R.11) and climbed from there by its NW ridge (II) in 1-1h30, turning one difficult tooth W and another E between a forepeak and main top. Another possibility is along E ridge from the Gaisskogel. This is reached from the Gubener hut via the Finstertal Alm and the Wannenkar, finally turning N to the top. After the Gaisskogel follow the dull ridge, II. About 4h.

Mittagsturm 2929m   **Mittagskopfe** 2934m   2895m

Zwölferkogel 2988m   Secondary rocky summits on ridge falling from the Sulzkogel towards Kühtai. Relatively easy approaches are available for all though they lack interest. The Zwölferkogel is the impressive looking mountain due S of Kühtai village.

SULZKOGEL 3016m

Situated just N of the Gamezkogel as a N projection of the Hoch-reichkopf-Kraspesspitze ridge. Excellent summit views and very popular with walkers.

Ordinary Route. Through varied scenery much changed since the construction of the Finstertal dam; the resultant mass of water now covers the area of the original small lakes. A chair-lift, the Drei-Seen, from Kühtai to just over 2300m at Ob. Plenderle avoids the walk below and up to the dam wall. F-. FA. A.Ledl, F.Stolz, 1899.

167 From the chairlift follow broad path to top of the Finster-tal dam. (If not using the lift, a path leaves Kühtai village run-ning down over the open hillside to the Finstertalbach, then climbing in the general direction of the E side of the dam, join-ing the road higher up. You can reach the same pt. using the surfaced road for all or part of the way, starting at the carpark by the Drei-Seen Lift).
Now follow E bank of the lake closely, a dull stony path. Soon after leaving the southern end of the lake note the Finstertal-scharte path branching L (R.16). The Sulzkogel is well signed and waymarked from here. Cross the stream and follow the W branch until crossing back L over both streams and ascending a rocky step L of a waterfall. Then zigzag up through boulders to edge of residual snow and rocks of the Gamezkogelferner (1h30). Follow N edge of the snowfield aiming for gap S of the summit and turn R up the marked route to top. Suitable for all and a nice ascent with super views (2h30 from chairlift).

North Ridge. Splendid though rarely done rock climb on a short but steep ridge, studded with numerous rock teeth, starting from the saddle S of the Mittagsturm. After the first tooth the ridge becomes knife-edged and occasionally overhanging. Higher up turn 3 teeth L though rock on the flanks is quite loose; it all becomes easier near the top. III+. Allow 1h30-2h for the ridge, about 4h30 from Kühtai.
A traverse along the ridge to the Gamezkogel is II.

Gamezkogel 2960m Easily climbed via its N ridge in 20 min. from the col pt.2920. Traverse to the Östl. Gamezkogel is easy (I) but of no importance.

Kraspesspitze 2953m As mentioned in the introduction to this section, an important topographical pt. Easily ascended from just S of the Finstertaler Scharte (see R.16) by its SW flank on an indistinct path; about 3h30 from huts. A traverse to the Schöllekogel is a little harder, sometimes II, in about 45 min.

ZWISELBACHER ROSSKOGEL   N 3060m   S 3082m

The N peak rises just above the SW corner of the Kraspesfer-
ner. The S peak is an attractive little rock pyramid (wrongly
called Gleirscher Rosskogel on AV map - this is actually a pt.
3008 on the S shoulder).

168 Normal Route from North. Pleasant with a possible variation being slightly more difficult, F. From Haggen in the
Sellraintal walk SW along the Kraspestal, up the step at c1920m
and past a small hut bearing the sign of a reporting centre for
mountain accidents. Here there is a marked path W for the Ste-
intalsattel and Kühtai. Soon cross the stream and climb E then
SW, all clearly marked, to pass E of the unattractive Kraspes
See. Keep L (E) of a prominent rocky shoulder and up onto the
glacier. The usual route leads W then SW, skirting edge of the
glacier to easy rocks and the N peak. Descend a little over
rocky ground before scrambling and walking easily in 10 min. to
the main S peak (4h).
An interesting alternative is to take the small glacier snout more
or less directly up its W side (some crevasses) to emerge on a
small fairly flat snowfield just SW of the Rotgrubenspitze, F+.
The descent to the Pforzheimer hut lies on the S border of this
snowfield at pt.2958. This area is quite confusing in mist and
from the S summit navigation to pt.2958 needs care. In this
respect ÖK 2705 is much clearer and includes an important landmark, a small pond just N of pt.2926.

169 Southern approach. From Pforzheimer hut follow R.25 initially before heading up into the Walfeskar, following the stream,
no path. From c2600m turn R (N) trending towards top of the
Pforzheimergrat. Nearer the top of this cirque there is an obvious escape L though a small col. This is pt.2958 though again,
in mist, it may be difficult to locate. Then navigate across another small col pt.2966 and loop round across snow and rocks to
approach the S peak from its N side - that is from the depression between N and S peaks which is also traversed on the
Haggen apporach as above (2h30). This is a much less interesting way than R.168.

South Ridge. FA. L.Purtscheller, J.Schnaiter, 1881. Some
pleasant pitches up to grade III. Reached via the Gleirschjöchl (see R.25), where a small track leads NW then N over 2
flattish shoulders to foot of the Gleirscher Rosskogel - see note
in R.168 about true location of this. Afterwards the ridge is
taken more or less directly over knolls, teeth and an occasional
deep gap, the last one being immediately before the summit (c4h
from either Pforzheimer or Gubener huts).

ROTGRUBENSPITZE (GRUBENKARSPITZE)   3040m

Rock pyramid rising steeply from SE corner of the Kraspesfer-
ner. Several possible routes: SW ridge from pt.2947 (II), NE

ridge from Rotgrubenscharte pt.2843 (III), and a traverse from the Zwiselbacher Rosskogel in about 2h.

The Pforzheimergrat, the ridge between the Walfeskar and the Rotgrube, is a recommended rock climb with a few pitches of IV above pt.2876 and about 5h from Pforzheimer hut. It must be said that the approach makes the shortish amount of good rock climbing hardly worthwhile.

Haidenspitze 2973m   More of a ridge than an individual peak, steep rock and scree tumbling down into the Kraspestal; grassy slopes and boulders to the E. Can be climbed from all sorts of directions - the SW ridge from the Rotgrubenscharte is IV in places and is the most logical. However all the routes lack real character.

Lampsenspitze 2875m   Small peak on ridge between the Gleirschtal and the Lisensertal just N of the Satteljoch and easily climbed from there: c3h30 from Praxmar and 1h30 from Pforzheimer hut (see note in hut details). The long N-running ridge to Freihut is an excellent excursion with good views though not greatly Alpine. Occasional pitches of II, takes about 4h.

Zischgelesspitze 3005m   Easy scramble from Praxmar in summer though chiefly a skier's mountain. The marked path goes SW along N side of the Moarler Bach with a short excursion N into a basin called the Sattelloch before turning W and SW to N ridge, thence to the summit, I (4h). It is also possible to make a round trip on a marked path by leaving the mountain along its E ridge; quit the ridge S before pt.2767 (Oberstkogel). After rounding the latter S the path goes over the Drei Zaiger pt. 2388 and the Köllenzaiger pt.2226 before running NE back into Praxmar.

An ascent from Pforzheimer hut through the Wildes Karl is tedious and the shattered connecting ridge to the Schöntalspitze (II) of very loose rock in parts is not recommended.

Schöntalspitze 3008m   Small rock peak E of the Zischgenscharte, an easy scramble (I) from the col itself and mostly waymarked, taking 10 min. There is even a summit book.

HINTERE GRUBENWAND   3175m   VORD. 3165m

The most southerly summits on long ridge between the Gleirschtal and the Lisensertal, separating the Gleirschferner from the more eastern and smaller Zischgelesferner. The Vord. peak is a sharp rock pyramid joined to the Hint. by a jagged ridge. The former's N ridge is IV and climbed via the Zischgelesferner (locally often called Zischgenferner), up to pt.2970, the first knoll on the ridge, then over the sharp and serrated continuation to the top, turning one tower R (W).

Vord. Peak – North-East Ridge. The usual way, sometimes coupled with a traverse to the Hint. top which is PD; otherwise F. FA. J.Pircher, R.Kreisel, L.Prochaska, 1894.

170   (a)   From Pforzheimer hut go down the Satteljoch path SE to cross over the Gleirsch stream. Soon afterwards turn S on L bank of the stream where the Satteljoch path turns E. Apart from a small kink at c2400m it ascends somewhat E of S to the Zischgelesferner. Continue in same line towards the Zischgenscharte (2917m), marked by a large cairn (3h).
    (b)   From the Westfalenhaus go NW, breaking off R from the Winnebachsee hut route at c2340m and passing Münsterhöhe (a well known viewpoint) to a small plateau above 2520m. The marked path then heads NNW into a small cirque. Take the R-hand gully (marked) steeply over scree and/or snow to the Zischgenscharte (1h30-2h).
Initially stay on the glacier and climb snow to gap in NE ridge at pt.3005 (coming from Pforzheimer hut make directly for it). Climb broken crest without difficulty, II (1h).
The short traverse to the Hintere peak takes 30 min. but is delicate and loose (III). After starting down the ridge take ledges on S side, finally climbing steep slabs to the top.

Completing a traverse of the 2 peaks from NE to SW involves a descent of the tricky SW ridge, some 2 km long from the Rosskarscharte to summit. In fact in descent you leave the ridge, which to this pt. has been taken direct over several towers; go down a steep loose and quite difficult gully R (N), situated just before (E of) 2 slabby pinnacles. This is also used in ascent, III/IV; allow 10h for the traverse and return to the Pforzheimer.

GLEIRSCHER FERNERKOGEL   3194m

Triangular snow roof at head of the Gleirscherferner and once known as the Rosskarspitze. It has a very steep rock wall on the W. Not climbed often; the normal route from the E is, in reverse, part of R.171 – the Sonnenwände traverse (4-5h, F).

SONNENWÄNDE

Östl. (unnamed on AV map) 3104m   Vord. 3159m   Mittl. 3111m   Hint. 3112m   Südl. 3094m

Long rock ridge comprising 5 tops of little individual significance with the exception of the distinguished Vordere peak which offers one of the best climbs in the vicinity. The Hint. and Südl. are easily climbed by their NE glacier slopes. The best expedition is to traverse the lot N to S, ending optionally with the Gleirscher Fernerkogel. Some loose rock should not deter. For those wishing a shorter outing the traverse can easily be abandoned at the Hint. or Südl. summits. Other variations might include addition of the Zwiselbacher Griesskogel (see below) or starting with the excellent NE ridge of the Vord. peak (R.172)

SONNENWÄNDE   NE side

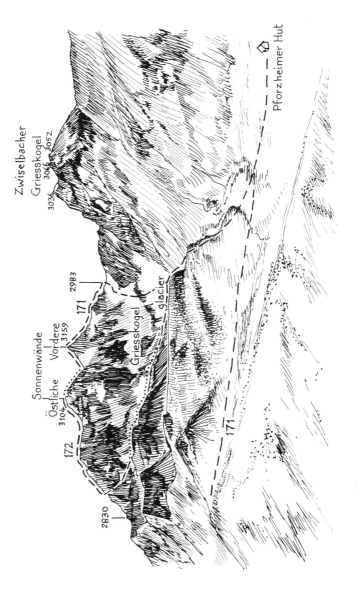

Zwiselbacher
Griesskogel
3036 3066 3052

Sonnenwände
Östliche
3104
172
2830

2983
171
Vordere
3159

Griesskogel
glacier
171

Pforzheimer Hut

171 Sonnenwände Traverse. PD. FA. L.Prochaska, F.Stolz,
H.Delago, 1897. Leave the Pforzheimer hut S across the Kuh-
warte in the direction of the Gleirschferner, heading SW from
the area called In den Samerschlägen via a small re-entrant
across grass and scree to remains of the Griesskogelferner,
continuing up to pt.2983, the saddle between the Zwiselbacher
Griesskogel and the Vord. Sonnenwand (2h). Climb latter by
its NW ridge, sometimes keeping L of difficulties on snow or
rocks (1h, 3h from hut).
Now the straightforward ridge leads S past trig. pt.3132 and
beyond this use scree ledges just below and R (W) of crest
where necessary to the indistinct Mittl. peak (45 min.). Now
round an obvious pinnacle on its R to a small scree platform;
continue along ridge to the Hint. peak (30 min.). Subsequently
the ridge becomes jagged. Cross a scree saddle and descend
a messy gully R of the crest before moving L back to it; then
go down 30m L towards the Südl. Sonnenwandferner and round
the next few towers on scree ledges to regain the ridge at a
pt. where it rises only slightly above the glacier which is then
used to avoid any further difficulties along to the Südl. peak
(1h30). The ridge to the Gleirscher Fernerkogel has some bits
of III but snow slopes on the L (E) side provide an easy route
(45 min., 6-6h30 from hut).
In descent keep near N ridge at first. About 50m below the
summit go E down the snow slope until some short snow gullies
drop to the SW corner of the Gleirscherfer. Take the L-hand
one (stonefall danger) and head ENE and later NNE down the
glacier, then over scree and grass slopes on W side of the valley. Keep N from c2500m and aim to pick up the path correctly
marked on AV map as disappearing S of the small lakes - Bei
den Seelen. From here there is a good path to the hut. Allow
9-10h for the whole round trip.

Vord. Peak - North-East Ridge. Splendid rock climb, AD, a
few pitches III, one of IV.

172   As for R.171 towards the Griesskogelferner; just below
it go SE to join the NE ridge above its lowest shoulder pt.2830.
Climb steep slabs (IV) to reach crest near 3 teeth (2h). Follow
ridge easily to 2 pinnacles, one turned L, the next R, to where
the crest narrows to a knife edge. Some slab pitches lead to
a short steep step followed by a long level section. The ridge
now rises to the Östl. peak 3104m, reached via a groove. Descend ridge to a small gap, turning a tower on slabs R. Climb
down the sharp edge beyond (5m, III) and continue over 2
teeth to the main saddle below the Vord. peak. From here go
up directly to summit (5h, 7h from Pforzheimer hut).

ZWISELBACHER GRIESSKOGEL   3066m

The S ridge rises gently from pt.2983 (see R.171); 2 prominent
pinnacles are turned L to reach pt.3036 via a smooth slab (II).

Then keep just below crest on W flank until a small gully leads back to crest and the summit (1h for ridge, 3h from Pforzheimer hut). It can also be climbed by the NW ridge from an area called the Stube, starting at a saddle S of pt.2627 and staying mostly on the ridge or just below on its W side, II (about 5h). The harder NE ridge starts from the Breite Scharte: turn the first tower R then climb steeply to lower summit and easily to the top (III).

WINNEBACHER WEISSKOGEL   3185m

Small rocky top easily climbed over snow from the Winnebachjoch (R.59). Excellent viewpoint, well worth a diversion during a transfer from Winnebachsee to Westfalen huts. No technical difficulties. The mountain looks much more impressive, even daunting, from the S and the W wall also is very steep.

173 Normal route. F. Equally easy from both huts, see above. From Winnebachjoch go N across boulders and snow. (Note an incorrect contour height on AV map, 2000 instead of 2900). After clearing 2900m turn W, passing either N or S of outcrop pt.2993, onto the small Weisskogelferner and aim for gap in N ridge at pt. 3160 just below summit. Take a final short steepish bit of snow before rather loose rock scrambling attains the top (1h from col).

Zwiselbacher Weisskogel 2961m   More a bump on the ridge between the Zwiselbach Joch and Winnebacher Weisskogel; easily bagged from the former in 45 min.

LARSTIGSPITZE   3173m

Pointed horn with slabby walls and ridges; poor rock detracts considerably from the climbing. The best route is probably the SW ridge from the Larstigscharte pt.3032; it is quite jagged and loose; generally stay on crest and turn any difficulties on S side, II (45 min.). This is preferable to the even looser SE ridge from the Zwiselbach Joch (see R.24) which is also a little harder. From the col go along the Griesskogelferner under the ridge until the latter steepens; then onto the ridge itself over an almost vertical step to a sharp bend in ridge S of summit. From here it is easier but not essential to take the rather loose L flank to top, II/III (1h30 from col).

From the Larstigspitze a ridge almost 7 km long, the Larstiggrat, leads N over a number of subsidiary summits finishing at the Sömenspitze. A traverse would finish (or start) at the Sömenscharte, easy of access from the Gubener hut. It is a serious undertaking, AD/D with pitches of IV, though difficulties are over by the Nördl. Larstigknotenspitze when travelling N. The round trip from the Gubener hut needs 14-15h.

Larstigfernerkopf 3216m   Unnamed on AV map, small but rather elegant rock pyramid between the Larstigspitze and Strahlkogel. From the Larstigscharte, III. To the S a ridge leads towards the Breiter Griesskogel on which lies another rocky knoll pt.3204.

STRAHLKOGEL   3295m

Considered one of the most beautifully formed mountains in the Stubai Alps, a large pyramid with a slender pointed rocky top. The name is derived from "Strahl" meaning ray or beam and refers to the obvious and wide horizontal quartz bands on the S-facing wall. It is remote, quite serious and not climbed often. A particularly early FA : P.C.Thurwieser in 1833, though his route is not recorded. He probably took the S flank which is the easiest way up (II), more or less in the summit fall line though sometimes W of it. It is steep and the rock is often loose; not recommended.

West Ridge. Ordinary route, PD+. In addition to approaches given below, the start pt. for the climb on the Grasstallferner can also be reached via the Grasstall or Larstig valleys to the N, or from Gries in Sulztal via the Salchenscharte. These alternatives would make the whole route rather longer, 5-6h to start of climb proper. FA. F.Drasch, L.Purtscheller, 1887.

174   The Zwiselbach Joch is reached from the Winnebachsee or Gubener huts by R.24. Ascend W over the Griesskogelferner to gap at pt.3148 just R (N) of the rocky knoll pt.3204. Descend the gentle upper slopes of the Grasstallferner WNW to arrive below the saddle between the Grasstaller Griesskogel and Strahlkogel, slightly nearer to the former (1h30). Scramble up scree gullies and over large blocks to saddle. The first ridge section is almost level and may be easier just below the crest R (S). Rejoin the ridge by a chimney and follow it steeply and sometimes exposed to summit (III). On one bit only can difficulties be turned R (3-3h30 from Zwiselbach Joch, 5h from the Winnebachsee hut, 6h30 from Gubener hut).

South-East ridge. Slightly harder than W ridge but somewhat shorter approach. AD-. FA. M.Pfaundler, G.Kunzel, 1899.

175   As for R.174 to pt.3148. Then go NNW across the Grasstallferner to a snow saddle c3170m NW of the Larstigfernerkopf pt.3216. Climb the first step directly (a few slab pitches). After this avoid the second and third steps L (S) then climb directly to the top (2h for ridge, 4h30-5h from Winnebachsee hut, 6h from the Gubener).

Other climbs. NE ridge, approached from the Larstigtal and the W bank of the Larstigferner; IV,rarely done. The N wall, over 400m high, has pitches of IV+ and is prone to stonefall.

Don't worry — I can easily see the hut from here.

GRASSTALLER GRIESSKOGEL   3160m

Rock peak on the westerly continuation of the Strahlkogel ridge
with impressive W and NE walls. The E ridge is easily climbed
(I) from the saddle noted in R.174 (30 min.).
The NW ridge is III, starting easily from the Kreuzjöchle pt.
2643 and over both the Grasstaller Köpfe pt.2942 and 3109; it
then gets harder and some difficulties can be turned L. From
the Kreuzjöchle, 3-4h.

Neederkogel 2756m   Northernmost rocky summit on the ridge
dividing the Larstigtal from the Grasstalltal. Rather a nice top,
easily reached in 45 min. from the Kreuzjöchle, itself attained by
a path up the Larstigtal from the Larstighofe.

Hemerkogel 2760m   Rocky top reached by a path from the
Ötztal just N of Längenfeld. No difficulties or merit.

Horndle 2986m   The SW outpost of the NW Stubai group. The
peak has narrow ridges to the N, E and SW with steep walls NW
and S. The N ridge (Vier-Zaiger-Grat) is quite hard (IV),more
so because of the 4 eponymous towers. Easier ascents are from
the SW (from Längenfeld, easy but 5h) and along the E ridge
from the Salchenscharte (also from Längenfeld, 5h30). Neither
offer great interest.

BREITER GRIESSKOGEL   3287m

Lovely snow peak S of Strahlkogel and the Grasstallferner on
the SW running subsidiary ridge finishing at Horndle. Excellent
viewpoint; the mountain is seen particularly well from the direction of the Winnebachjoch. FA. L.Purtscheller, F.Schnaiter,1881.

176 Ordinary Route. Straightforward snow climb, F. Reach
the Zwiselbach Joch from the Winnebachsee or Gubener huts by
R.24. Now go onto the glacier keeping to its southern limits
past the small icefall where the gradient steepens. Above
c3140m work R to approach summit from the NE. It is possible
to take a much more direct line to the top but each year the
snow cover diminishes and there are underlying polished slabs
as well as some large holes to fall onto (1-1h30 from the Joch,
about 3-3h30 from Winnebachsee hut, 4-4h30 from the Gubener).

177 From Niederthai. An unconventional approach, and longer,
from the valley, F. FA. F.Plaseller, E.Seherka, F.Karlinger,
1896. After leaving Niederthai up the Horlach valley turn S
into the Grasstalltal as far as the Grasstallsee. Then take a
small scree filled valley NNE, up to the steep tongue and moraine
of the Grasstallferner to the flatter snowfield above. Continue
E and underneath the NE ridge before turning sharply S to join
R.176 (5h).

GÄNSEKRAGEN   2915m

Small rocky peak W of the Winnebachsee hut, easily reached on a marked path from hut in c2h; you crest the ridge just NW of the summit.
The E ridge is a nice straightforward rock climb with about 3 pitches of III, the rest being easier. It is best to leave the hut N on R.24 and turn W at or just before the first junction/signpost. Go up over grassy and rocky slopes to foot of the ridge and follow crest to top; 2 deviations are required, both to the R (N); the first just before the first levelling out of the ridge about 100m from the start, the second to turn an obvious hump before the final steepening (3h).

HOHER SEEBLASKOGEL   3235m

Impressive peak looming above the Westfalenhaus with an interesting variety of climbs from all points of the compass.

178 Normal Route. Straightforward and not without interest, F. FA. G.Holzknecht, F.Plaseller, 1897. From Winnebachsee hut follow R.61 up onto N side of the Bachfallenferner. At c2680 a small signposted path veers L away from the directionally indicated R.61 Gaisslehnscharte route and gradually turns NE up scree into the area called Grüne Tatzen – Green Claw pressumably because of a small curved area of grass growing twixt the rocks; continue NW up a narrow valley to join the SW ridge overlooking the Grüne Tatzen glacier to the E; this latter section was clearly marked with red/white signs in 1988. Now either stay on ridge and traverse 2 rocky humps to summit or, easier, move down onto the glacier which rises almost onto the ridge itself at gap pt.3102 and join R.180 (3h).

179 North-West ridge. Complex crest which changes direction twice; a long rock climb from the Winnebachjoch. AD, not sustained, recommended locally. From Westfalen or Winnebachsee huts use R.59 to the Winnebachjoch (1h30). Climb directly to the first shoulder, Am Zoachen (2980m). This is best done direct though it is possible to move R and avoid some harder pitches. Then keep to crest over several teeth (II) to a steep step climbed by L edge (crux, III). Continue on ridge to pt. 3122, the second shoulder. Here the direction turns SE; a lesser branch forks SW (ignore). Continue along the now easier crest over blocks to the top (5h from either hut).

180 Grüne Tatzen Ferner route. An interesting climb, F. From Westfalen hut take R.4 (Dr Siemons Weg) SW then S towards the Längentaler Ferner. At c2420m a small signposted path branches WSW through boulders then up quite steep scree to the concealed Grüne Tatzen Ferner. Some danger of stonefall in the ensuing narrow and steep glacier entrance; higher up the snowfield the gradient eases. Aim for the ridge between pt.3171 to the R(E) and the summit L. Danger - do not go right up to this apparent snow ridge - there is usually a cornice overhanging a steep snow gully. Instead move L to foot of the easy and short E ridge and in a few min. reach the top (3h30 from hut).

Another possibility for this peak is by way of the NE ridge (Ochsenkargrat), leading from the Fuchsgrat (2728m) up to the E shoulder pt.3171, PD+.

BACHFALLENKOPF   3176m

Rock peak at head of a small southward pointing extension of the eastern Bachfallenferner and rising W above the Längentalerferner. Seldom climbed in its own right but in fact quite interesting and pleasant. Straightforward in 3h from the Winnebachsee hut, from R.61 at c2780m and climbing steeply up the glacier tongue, keeping L (E) and getting onto the ridge just E of the summit. Traverse to the Längentaler Weisser Kogel is II in 45 min. down the ridge to a saddle, then mostly up snow to top.

LÄNGENTALER WEISSER KOGEL   3218m

Snow peak at head of the Längentalerferner. The easiest route is a glacier walk from the Westfalen hut using R.4 initially, then heading SW just on the N side of the Längentaljoch. Next up the snowfield to the saddle between the Weisser Kogel and Bachfallenkopf and up the easy ridge to top, F (3h from Westfalen hut, 4h from the Amberger). It can also be climbed from the Bachfallenferner and Winnebachsee hut using a scrappy and stonefall prone gully to the easy N ridge, F (3h from hut). The ridge from the Gaisslehnscharte (R.61) is harder (III) with some loose rock.

Gaisslehnkogel group   Östl. 3216m   Westl. 3213m   Kleiner 3145m

This collection of peaks forms the southernmost boundary of the Bachfallenferner. The higher more easterly top (II) takes 45 min. using the NE ridge from the Gaisslehnscharte. In descent (it can of course be used for ascent) take the E ridge for 200m (II), then break R down into the Schrankar towards small lake at 2688m.

Kühlehnkarschneide   S 3196m   N 3188m   Easily (I) from the Kühlenkarscharte pt.3012 in 30 min. to the S peak using a route over boulders R of the summit fall line. The ridge itself is slightly harder (II). It is another 30 min. to the N peak (II).

PUTZENKARSCHNEIDE   Vord. 3120m   Hint. 3073m

2 peaks lying between the Bachfallenferner E, the tiny Putzenkarferner N and the Säuischbachferner W.

181 From North. Quick and straightforward, F. From Winnebachsee hut by R.61 to small lake at 2485m. Here turn SE at a
signpost for the Putzenkarscharte, through the Putzenkarle. So
to the Putzenkarferner, then veer SW to the col itself pt.2902.
Now to the Vord. summit SE along the ridge, I+ (3h from hut).

All the peaks from the Gaisslehnscharte to the Putzenkarschneide
can be more or less directly traversed at II.

Winnebachspitzen   Hohe 3155m   Niedere 3054m and 2992m
Vord. 2827m   Small tops enclosing the Säuischbachferner W
and S. All can be climbed from the glacier itself without much
interest.

Appendix

TWO TALES OF THE STUBAI

The Franz Senn hut

This was not the first hut to be built in the region, being preceded by the Dresdner (1875) and the Innsbrucker (1884), but it has become the largest certainly in size and probably in importance.

Pastor Franz Senn was born in Längenfeld in the Ötztal and pioneered the idea of tourism in that area in an attempt to alleviate the considerable poverty around his first parish in Vent. He then moved to Nauders where he spent some unhappy years before working in Neustift until his death in 1884 aged 52 years. It was he who originally suggested the building of a hut in the Alpeinertal and he was an important patron of both the ÖAV and DAV. In 1885 the hut was opened by the DÖAV and named in his memory.

When originally built as a two-storey affair the hut had 12 Matratzenlager places on the ground floor (of which 4 were reserved for ladies) and 8 places plus a hayloft on the first floor. Wooden barriers were placed between each Matratzen place in order that the proprieties of the day might be preserved. Some may feel that this is a custom which is long overdue for revival. By 1902 there were already marked routes to all the major peaks round the valley and it was recorded that there were 693 visitors to the hut in 1905. In 1907 the path from Oberiss Alm was constructed thereby bringing the Alpeinerferner within reach of the day-tripper. Newspaper advertisements of the time suggested taking the Stubaitalbahn to Fulpmes with a carriage ride onwards to Oberiss. Not surprisingly with this popularity, the further enlargement of the hut in 1909 to 50 places (and a bigger hayloft) included a guides' room. Yet another extension in 1932-33 introduced electricity and 150 places. During the 2nd war the hut was closed to climbers and used by the German Army for training. Their engineers installed the Materialseilbahn from Oberiss to the hut now used for supplies and rucksacks. Even larger capacity resulted from more building in 1954-55 and again in 1960 to the almost 250 places currently available.

An Ascent of the Ruderhofspitze by B. Lergetporer

On 7th July 1874 I left Neustift at 2.30 in the afternoon with my two guides Friedrich Jenewein and Matthias Schönherr and walked up the Oberberg valley. The weather was very promising. By 6.45 we had reached Ober-Iss Alp where we found friendly accommodation.

When I stepped outside the following morning the sky was for the most part covered with dark clouds and the prevailing south

wind did not suggest an improvement. At 3.30am we left Ober-
Iss in somewhat low spirits. Scarcely had half an hour passed,
and whilst we were climbing steeply towards the Alpeiner Alp,
when it began to rain. We sheltered under a fir tree. After a
short wait the rain stopped and by 5.30 we were on the Alpeiner
glacier. In spite of the early season snow many rocks were appearing and so after a short march up the glacier we crossed to
the enormous right bank moraine and for 45 minutes ascended
along it. The south wind had by now moderated and the prev-
iously threatening clouds were breaking up. When we left the
moraine and got onto the snow we roped up and turned west to
circumvent the glacier icefall and so reach the upper snowfield.
On the right lay the Schwarzenberger Joch and the dramatic
Schrankogel, on the left reigned the majestic and peaceful Ruderhofspitze.

Until now we had followed the same route as Dr von Ruthner and
Carl Bädeker on the first ascent of the Ruderhofspitze on 29
August 1864. These gentlemen, after traversing the upper snowfield leftwards, had climbed to the peak over a steep snow slope
and then over snow covered rocks. I was certain that this bit
of rock climbing was not going to be a pleasant experience. So
we proceeded directly to a saddle between the Hölltalspitze and
Ruderhofspitze, later to be useful in our descent to Mutterberg
Alp. At 10.15 we reached the saddle without difficulty and had
a short rest.

I do not know whether this col had a name. It seemed appropriate to call it the Hölltalscharte. After a break of some twenty
minutes we set off again upwards. To begin with we turned a
steep rock pitch on the snowfield but then stayed on the ridge
almost all the way to the summit. Although the ridge was entirely covered with soft snow and in some places overhanging on
the Alpeiner glacier side, generally there were no problems. On
a prominent rock we saw a pole placed there for surveying purposes and by 12.15pm we had conquered the peak.

*

This was in fact the first ascent of Ruderhofspitze from the
Hölltalscharte though this saddle had been crossed in 1863 by
J.A. Specht. The party descended to Mutterberg Alm where
they rested for a day before climbing Zuckerhütl by the Lange
Pfaffennieder, returning through Mutterberg Alm down the Stubaital to Ranalt. The following morning, 10th July, Lergetporer
and the guide Jenewein left Ranalt at 4am and walked up the
Langental, through the small gorge up to Grübl Alm and then
up to the Grübl glacier which he called the Langenthalferner.
After a short diversion over the lower rocks of Hochgrintl the
pair crossed over onto the Feuersteinferner using the Enges
Türl, even then recognised by several authors as difficult from
the north, through the Hoher Trog and down into the Ridnauntal. After a refreshment pause in Ridnaun they continued
on to Sterzing, arriving at 6.35pm.

Index

155